Machine and Hand
Joinery

Machine and Hand Joinery

The Editors of
Fine Woodworking

The Taunton Press

 The Taunton Press

The Taunton Press, Inc., 63 South Main Street, PO Box 5506, Newtown, CT 06470-5506
e-mail: tp@taunton.com

Jacket/Cover design: Susan Fazekas
Interior design: Susan Fazekas
Layout: Cathy Cassidy
Front cover photographer: ©Donna Chiarelli
Back cover photographers: (clockwise from top left) Mark Schofield, ©The Taunton Press, Inc.;
Jonathan Binzen, ©The Taunton Press, Inc.; Vincent Laurence, ©The Taunton Press, Inc.

The New Best of Fine Woodworking® is a trademark of The Taunton Press, Inc.,
registered in the U.S. Patent and Trademark Office.
Library of Congress Cataloging-in-Publication Data

Machine and hand joinery / the editors of Fine woodworking.
    p. cm. -- (The new best of fine woodworking)
 ISBN-13: 978-1-56158-856-5
 ISBN-10: 1-56158-856-3
 1. Furniture making. 2. Joinery. I. Fine woodworking II. Series.
 TT194.M285 2006
 684'.08--dc22

                    2006011271

Printed in the United States of America
10 9 8 7 6 5 4 3 2 1

The following manufacturers/names appearing in *Machine and Hand Joinery* are trademarks:
Elu™, JDS Multi-Router®, Leigh FMT Jig®, MatchMaker®, Ryobi® Woodcarver,
Woodtek®.

Working wood is inherently dangerous. Using hand or power tools improperly or ignoring
safety practices can lead to permanent injury or even death. Don't try to perform operations
you learn about here (or elsewhere) unless you're certain they are safe for you. If something
about an operation doesn't feel right, don't do it. Look for another way. We want you to enjoy
the craft, so please keep safety foremost in your mind whenever you're in the shop.

Acknowledgments

Special thanks to the authors, editors, art directors, copy editors, and other staff members of *Fine Woodworking* who contributed to the development of the articles in this book.

Contents

Introduction

You can have the most beautiful wood and lovely design, but without rock-solid joinery, your furniture won't hold up. Joinery holds the structure together and allows the piece to be used and even a bit abused. Take dining chairs, for example. Although they have four legs, your guests may occasionally test their structure by leaning back so that only two legs of the chair support their entire weight. If you haven't built your chair with sufficient joint strength, your diners could end up on the floor in a heap of sticks.

The concept of joinery is as old as recorded history. Furniture with hand-cut dovetail joints has been found entombed with the mummies dating back to ancient Egypt. Several thousand years later, dovetails are still being used today to fasten objects of wood.

Fast forward to the 18th century, a period that is arguably the zenith of fine furniture making. The joints used—dovetails, mortise and tenons, and edge joints—are still the most predominant joints used today. And there are thousands and thousands of pieces from that era still being used today.

While the tools may have changed in the last two centuries, the concepts have not. We know a little more about how wood behaves—cross-grain joints,

for example, are risky unless the parts are narrow—and we now have better glues. But for the most part, you can still build furniture using the exact joinery employed by craftsmen dating back to Colonial times. As long as they are properly executed, your pieces will last into the next generation and beyond.

The most essential factors to strong joints are dry wood and close tolerances.

Whether you cut mortise and tenon joints with hand tools or craft them with machines, the same rules apply. In this book of articles reprinted from *Fine Woodworking* magazine, you'll learn the secrets to tight fitting joints using both traditional and modern tools.

When you fit together a well-crafted joint, the experience is as satisfying as putting on a pair of well-designed leather gloves. And the pride you feel will be appreciated by those who use your furniture and aren't relegated to a pratfall.

—Anatole Burkin, Editor-in-Chief
Fine Woodworking

A Lesson in Basic Joinery

BY MARIO RODRIGUEZ

My students always find it more satisfying to perfect their joinery by creating a piece of furniture rather than by adding to the kindling in the scrap bin. The dado and the rabbet are fundamental woodworking joints found in all kinds of furniture, from bookcases to highboys. Building this organizer, which either can be hung on a wall or stood on a table, allows you to practice these joints while creating a useful piece of furniture.

This piece features dadoes that run the width of the sides to support the shelves, and stopped dadoes in the upper shelf and the underside of the top to receive the partitions. Rabbets in the cabinet include those at the top of each sidepiece and partition as well as in the drawer construction. Both joints provide accurate alignment of the parts, load-bearing capability, and increased glue surface. They can be cut accurately on the tablesaw, with or without a dado set, and with a router using various fences and jigs.

Materials Are Cheap and Easy to Find

I chose red oak as the primary wood for this project and pine for the drawer boxes and the back slats. If you can find 11-in.-wide oak boards, you will be spared the step of gluing up panels, but glue-up is not a big procedure for a project this size. The oak for the partitions needs to be thicknessed to ½ in., and most of the pine needs to be ⅜ in. thick; this is best done with a planer rather than trying to resaw thicker stock. You will need about 18 ft. of 8-in.-wide oak boards, and 7 ft. of pine, which includes an extra 20 percent to be on the safe side.

Simple But Useful Joints

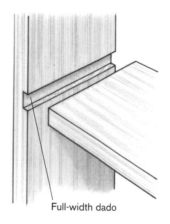
Full-width dado

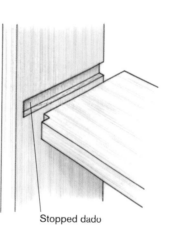
Stopped dado

Dadoes
The dado, a square, flat-bottomed recess cut across the grain of one board to receive the end of another, can run the full width of the board or stop short of one or both edges.

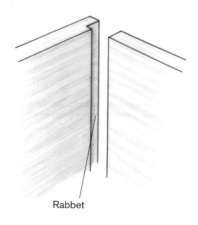
Rabbet

Rabbets
The rabbet is an open-sided recess cut along the edge or end of a board to receive the edge of another.

Small Storage Case Assembles Easily

Red oak is the primary wood for this project because it is handsome, hard wearing, and not difficult to work. Pine was used for the drawer boxes and the back slats. Both woods are readily available at home centers at a moderate price. Look for oak boards that are quarter-sawn (growth rings perpendicular to the face of the board) for a sleek, high-quality appearance. Most home-center lumber is milled to ¾-in. thickness, so the board's grain should be easy to see.

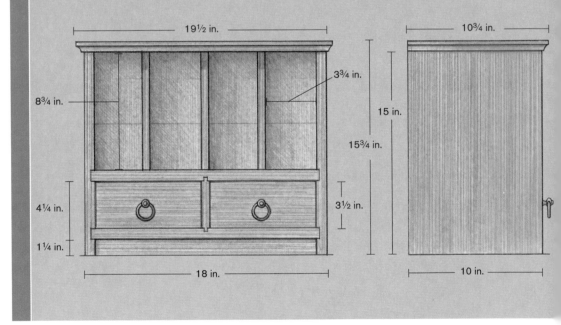

Dadoes and Rabbets Can Be Cut on the Tablesaw

Most of the dadoes and rabbets for this project can be cut on the tablesaw using a set of dado blades. There are two types of dado blades (see the photos on p. 8): stackable blades, which consist of two outside blades to cut the sides of the joint and multiple chipper blades to remove the waste in the middle, and adjustable blades, also known as wobble blades. I prefer the stackable dado set because it makes a cleaner cut. Install a throat insert made for a dado set. Mount the two outside blades and sufficient chippers to make a cut just under ¾ in. wide. Using a piece of surplus oak as a gauge to make test cuts, fine-tune the width

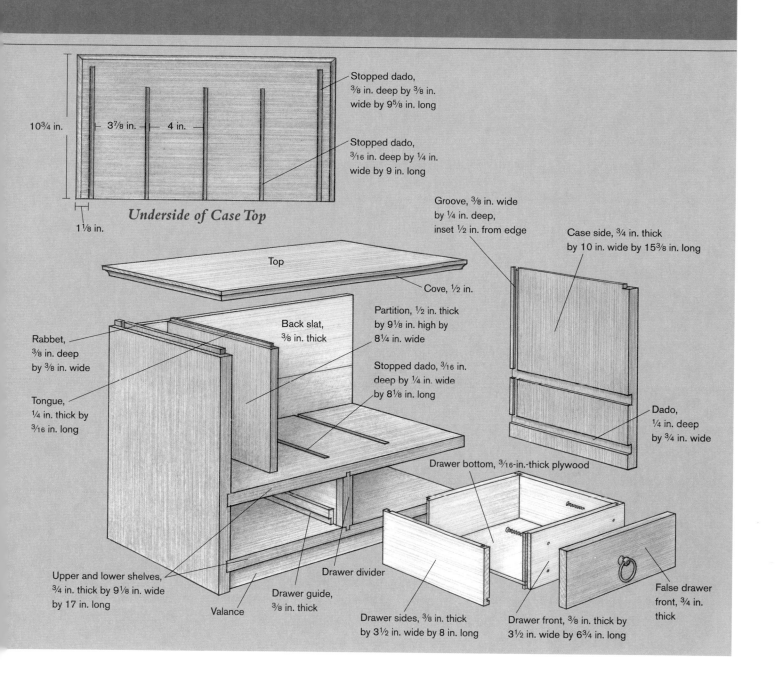

Stopped dado, ³⁄₈ in. deep by ³⁄₈ in. wide by 9⁵⁄₈ in. long

Stopped dado, ³⁄₁₆ in. deep by ¹⁄₄ in. wide by 9 in. long

10¾ in.

3⅞ in.   4 in.

1⅛ in.

Underside of Case Top

Groove, ³⁄₈ in. wide by ¹⁄₄ in. deep, inset ½ in. from edge

Case side, ¾ in. thick by 10 in. wide by 15³⁄₈ in. long

Top

Cove, ½ in.

Partition, ½ in. thick by 9⅛ in. high by 8¼ in. wide

Back slat, ³⁄₈ in. thick

Rabbet, ³⁄₈ in. deep by ³⁄₈ in. wide

Stopped dado, ³⁄₁₆ in. deep by ¹⁄₄ in. wide by 8⅛ in. long

Tongue, ¼ in. thick by ³⁄₁₆ in. long

Dado, ¼ in. deep by ¾ in. wide

Drawer bottom, ³⁄₁₆-in.-thick plywood

Upper and lower shelves, ¾ in. thick by 9⅛ in. wide by 17 in. long

Drawer divider

False drawer front, ¾ in. thick

Valance

Drawer guide, ³⁄₈ in. thick

Drawer sides, ³⁄₈ in. thick by 3½ in. wide by 8 in. long

Drawer front, ³⁄₈ in. thick by 3½ in. wide by 6¾ in. long

by adding or removing shims between the blades until you achieve a snug fit.

Each sidepiece gets a pair of dadoes for the shelves, and the top and bottom shelves each receive one narrow dado for the drawer divider. Dadoes shallower than ¼ in. deep can be cut in one pass, but feed the workpiece slowly to achieve a clean cut and avoid straining the motor. Use the rip fence

to guide the location of each dado, making the same cut on both sidepieces before adjusting the fence for the next dado. Apply firm downward pressure on the workpiece to ensure that the depth of each dado is consistent throughout its length.

Even though the cut for the rabbets on the top of each sidepiece is ³⁄₈ in. square, there is no need to reset the width of

Cut Full-Length Dadoes and Rabbets on the Tablesaw

TWO TYPES OF DADO BLADES ARE AVAILABLE. The outside cutters of a stackable set of blades (left) are placed on the arbor first and last, with chipper blades between them. The width of the cut is fine-tuned by placing metal or paper shims between the blades. Adjustable blades (below), also called wobble blades, can be adjusted to width by rotating a dial on the side of the blade.

Tablesaw fence

Dado blades

Workpiece

CUTTING A DADO. the depth of the dado should equal about a third of the wood's thickness. Apply constant pressure both against the fence and downward to ensure that the cut is consistent in depth across the piece. With narrow workpieces, use a miter gauge for guidance and support.

Tablesaw fence

Sacrificial fence

Workpiece

Dado blades

CUTTING A RABBET. After cutting the dadoes for the shelves, flip the board and cut the rabbet on the top of each side, creating a narrow tongue that will enter the top. To avoid damage to the rip fence, clamp on a sacrificial plywood fence.

A Quick Drawer Joint Made with Dadoes and Rabbets

CUT DADOES IN THE DRAWER SIDES. The positions of the dadoes on the drawer sides are determined by the thickness of the front and rear drawer pieces.

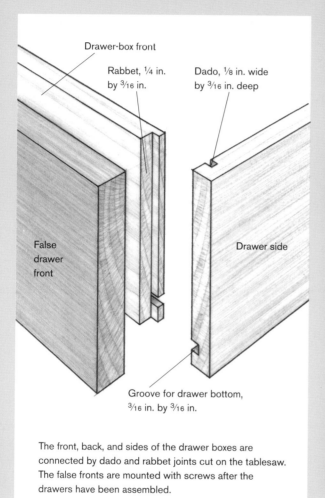

Drawer-box front

Rabbet, ¼ in. by ³⁄₁₆ in.

Dado, ⅛ in. wide by ³⁄₁₆ in. deep

False drawer front

Drawer side

Groove for drawer bottom, ³⁄₁₆ in. by ³⁄₁₆ in.

The front, back, and sides of the drawer boxes are connected by dado and rabbet joints cut on the tablesaw. The false fronts are mounted with screws after the drawers have been assembled.

RABBET THE FRONT and rear pieces in two steps. Move the front and rear drawer pieces vertically across the blade (left) to make the first part of the rabbet. Use a zero-clearance insert plate around the blade to support the workpiece. With the piece flat on the table (above), make the second cut, leaving a tongue that will connect with the side pieces.

the dado set. Instead, clamp a piece of ¾-in.-thick plywood or medium-density fiberboard (MDF) to the rip fence, locate the fence for the cut, and gradually raise the blade so that it eats into this sacrificial fence.

The final cuts with the dado blade are ⅛-in.-deep by ³⁄₁₆-in.-wide rabbets on both sides of each end of the three partitions, and ³⁄₁₆-in.-deep by ¼-in.-wide rabbets on overlapping sides of the pine back slats. Known as a shiplap joint, this allows the boards to move seasonally without creating a gap between them.

Stopped Dadoes Are Best Cut with a Router

On this project the partitions are secured in stopped dadoes in the upper shelf and the top.

The stopped dadoes must be cut in identical positions on the top shelf and the underside of the top piece. To achieve this I use a rub collar (also called a template guide) in conjunction with a template. The collar has a tubelike piece of metal that surrounds the router bit and guides it by means of a template placed on the workpiece. When laying out the job and making the router template, the difference between the outer diameter of the rub collar (in this case ⁹⁄₁₆ in.) and the router bit (¼ in.) must be taken into account. Blocks of wood glued to the underside of the template act as stops to ensure accurate placement on both of the pieces to be cut.

I also use the router to cut ⅜-in.-square stopped dadoes on the sides for the back slats and on the underside of the top for the sides. Because these cuts are near the edges of the workpiece, a fence attached to the router and guided by these edges works well. You will need to stop the router just before the end of each cut and square up the end with a chisel.

While you have the router out, now's a good time to profile the edge of the top. Although the piece shown here has a cove on the underside of the front and sides of the top piece, you may prefer the look of a chamfer. Regardless, use a bearing-guided bit running along the edge of the workpiece. For a clean cut with minimal tearout or burning, make the cut in two stages with the second cut at the final depth removing only a small amount of wood.

Cut the Drawer Parts Using the Tablesaw

Because the drawers have false fronts and are fitted with guides, it is safe to make up the drawer boxes before the carcase is

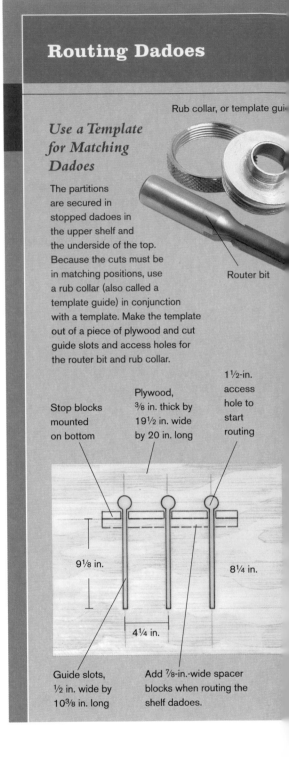

Routing Dadoes

Use a Template for Matching Dadoes

The partitions are secured in stopped dadoes in the upper shelf and the underside of the top. Because the cuts must be in matching positions, use a rub collar (also called a template guide) in conjunction with a template. Make the template out of a piece of plywood and cut guide slots and access holes for the router bit and rub collar.

Rub collar, or template guide

Router bit

Stop blocks mounted on bottom

Plywood, ⅜ in. thick by 19½ in. wide by 20 in. long

1½-in. access hole to start routing

9⅛ in.

8¼ in.

4¼ in.

Guide slots, ½ in. wide by 10⅜ in. long

Add ⅞-in.-wide spacer blocks when routing the shelf dadoes.

assembled. The front, back, and sides of the boxes are connected by dado and rabbet joints cut on the tablesaw: First cut two dadoes on each sidepiece; the distance from the end is determined by the thickness of the front and back pieces.

Because the next cut is made with only a thin section of wood in contact with

CUT THE TEMPLATE GUIDE. With a T-square guide clamped to the edge of the plywood template, rout a slot for the template guide to ride in.

ROUTER TEMPLATE SPACES PARTITIONS EVENLY. Because the stopped dadoes for the partitions must be cut precisely and in identical positions on both the upper shelf and the top, it is best to use a plywood template to guide the router.

THE TEMPLATE GUIDES THE ROUTER. A rub collar (or template guide) screwed to the router base runs against the template, guiding the router bit.

the tablesaw, install a zero-clearance insert around the sawblade to prevent the workpiece from getting wedged between the table and the blade. In two cuts you can make rabbets on the ends of the drawer back and sides to create a tongue that connects with the dadoes on the drawer sides. Before assembling the boxes, cut grooves on the inside of the front and sides, and cut away the back of the drawers so that the bottom can be slid in.

The drawer partition simply is a ¾-in.-thick piece of pine that is joined to the two shelves with ¼-in. dadoes. These can be cut on the tablesaw with two passes over a conventional blade. To avoid having end grain

An Edge Guide Is Another Option

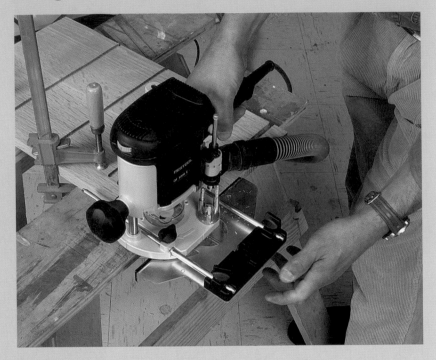

AFTER CUTTING THE STOPPED DADOES for the partitions, add an adjustable fence to the router and cut the stopped dadoes at both ends of the top to receive the sides.

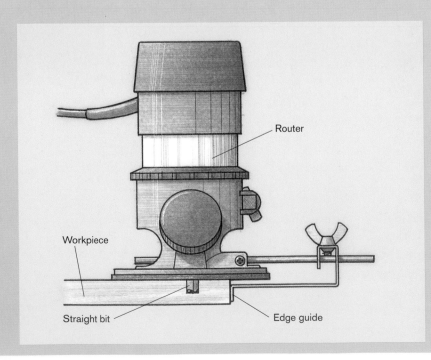

Router

Workpiece

Straight bit

Edge guide

exposed on the front of the cabinet, use a tongue-and-groove joint to attach a thin facing piece of oak.

Assemble the Carcase and Fit the Drawers

You will find that the assembly of this project will be much easier to do on a pair of sawhorses, because the gap between the horses allows more room for clamping. Glue the shelves to the cabinet sides and slide in the drawer divider from the front. When these joints are dry, slide in the back slats, glue in the three partitions, and then glue on the top. Screw the center of each back slat to the sides.

Before fitting the drawers, mill some rabbeted drawer guides from pine and set them in place with glue. The rabbet along the bottom and the fact that they are 1½ in. short allow them to be trimmed in place with a block plane.

Once you have achieved a snug fit for each drawer box, mark its location on the back of each false drawer front. Transfer the location of the holes on the drawer box and drill pilot holes in the false front to avoid splitting the wood with the screws.

The last pieces to add are a valance that is set in from the sides and glued to the lower shelf, and a two-part French cleat if you are going to hang the organizer on a wall. Before assembly you should sand the interior sections with 100-, 150-, and 220-grit paper. With the piece assembled, plane all of the joints flush and repeat the sanding sequence on the outside. Sand these areas again with 220-grit paper.

Finish the wood with three coats of an oil-varnish mixture, such as Waterlox, sanding between the first two coats with 220-grit paper. When the finish has cured, rub the cabinet with 0000 steel wool, and wax and buff the wood for a smooth, satin finish.

MARIO RODRIGUEZ is a contributing editor to *Fine Woodworking* magazine.

Construct the Case and Fit the Drawers

ASSEMBLE THE PIECE. Begin by gluing the sides to the two shelves. Apply some glue to the grooves and slide in the drawer divider from the front. Then slide in the back slats and glue in the partitions. The last piece of the case to be attached is the top. Working on a pair of sawhorses gives you more options for clamping positions.

DRAWER GUIDES have a rabbet and stop 1½ in. from the back slats. This allows the thickness to be trimmed with a block plane after they have been installed.

FIT THE DRAWER FRONTS. After cutting the false fronts to size, mark the location of the drawer box on the back of each, including the holes. To attach the drawer front, drill the holes in the drawer box slightly oversize to allow for fine-tuning to the opening.

Legs to Stand On

BY TIMOTHY S. PHILBRICK

Most of my furniture could be considered contemporary interpretations of classic forms. Though devoid of most ornament, the shapes, proportions, and subtle details all hail from classic pieces. But my joinery ranges from the strictly traditional (delicate half-blind dovetails to connect drawer fronts to sides) to the innovative. I use whatever joinery seems like it will best do the job, regardless of the era.

In this article, I will discuss a couple of techniques that I have developed and used successfully for years to attach legs to tables and carcases. These techniques take advantage of some technological advances in materials and joinery, such as plywood and biscuits, yet they respect and conform to some basic precepts of woodworking: Wood moves, and a piece of furniture must be functionally sound first and beautiful second.

I use two main types of legs, turned and shaped, the making of which I describe on pp. 16–17. Sometimes all four legs (or six on longer pieces) will be turned, but more often than not, I'll shape the front pair; on a piece with six legs, I'll shape the two inner legs (see the photo on p. 19). When viewed from the front, the shaped legs usually have the same profile as the turned legs, but as you move around the piece, the profile changes. By shaping the legs, I give a piece of furniture an orientation and, hopefully, some grace. I try to give my furniture a stance not unlike a ballet dancer.

The techniques for applying the legs are the same whether they are turned or shaped and differ only depending on whether you are attaching a corner leg or an inner leg. With both turned and shaped legs, it's best to cut your joinery first while

the blank is still square or rectangular. Although it is possible to cut the joinery after the legs have been turned or shaped, you would need to build rather sophisticated custom fixtures to hold the legs and would give yourself an unnecessary headache. Cut the joinery first.

AT FIRST GLANCE, all these legs appear turned. Closer inspection reveals the subtle asymmetrical shaping of the inner legs, giving the piece, a claro walnut sideboard, more interest and life. Regardless of shape, the author uses the same joinery techniques to apply the legs.

Preparing Turned and Shaped Legs

For both shaped and turned legs, I begin with a blank cut to exact length. If it's going to be an inner leg, I can use the tablesaw, a router table or my horizontal mortising machine to create the stopped mortise in the back of the leg. I always check a scrap of the same plywood I'm using for the partition to be sure that it fits tightly in the mortise. Plywood thickness is never exactly as advertised, so it's important to check every sheet.

If it's a corner leg for a table or a straightforward carcase piece, I can use any of the same machines, but I find it easiest to use the horizontal mortising machine. Often, on the pieces I build, a corner will not be a true 90°. Instead it will be 95° or 100° because the front bows forward, away from perpendicular with the sides. To compensate for this when using the slot mortiser, I cut wedges at the appropriate angle on the tablesaw and use them under the blank when I'm mortising. The result is a pocket or hollow of precisely the correct angle.

SHAPING LEGS

Generally, when I'm shaping legs for a piece of furniture, there are also turned legs on the piece. I use the template for the turned legs as the template for the front view of the shaped pieces. Then I mark out this profile on the piece to be shaped and bandsaw it out (see the drawing at right). Next I flip the blank onto its side, mark out the side profile from a template I've made for the shaped legs and bandsaw that out. It's not necessary to tape the offcuts from the first sawing back onto the blank to cut the side profile because the curves I work with are so gentle and subtle that the piece I'm sawing never really rocks. The next step is to locate the arris (the sharp leading edge of the legs). I do this by finding the centerpoints at the top and bottom of each leg from side to side and then taking a long, flexible rule and connecting the two points.

Now comes the tricky part. For this task, I've used a number of different tools over the years, from a boatbuilder's abrasive pad mounted on an electric drill, to the Ryobi® Woodcarver (no longer available), to drawknives, spokeshaves, and block planes. The idea is to create a fair, smooth curve over the length and across the breadth of each leg no matter how you look at it. I always finish up with rasps, files, and scrapers before going to sandpaper.

TURNING LEGS

Preparing a turned leg starts just the same as the shaped leg. I take a square blank of the correct length, and then I cut my joinery—either a stopped mortise or the corner pocket. Then things diverge. I check the joinery of the leg blank for fit, adjust it if necessary, and then I cut a plug or insert to fill the void where I mortised for the corner. (On all of my pieces these days, the inner legs are shaped.) The best wood for this plug is the same wood as your leg because it will turn and sand with the same resistance and at the same speed. Second best is a wood that is slightly softer and close to the same color.

I spot-glue the plug into the corner pocket, using two of the tiniest smears of glue imaginable, right into the inside corner of the pocket about an inch from the bottom and an inch from the top. Then, after waiting for the glue to dry, I trim off any excess plug so that the plug looks like it's part of the leg blank.

I find the centers of the blank at either end using a combination square, and then I mark a circle at both ends with a compass. I set my tablesaw blade at 45° and rip the blank into an octagon just outside the perimeter of the circles at each end. I turn, sand, and sometimes even finish on the lathe. Sanding can be tricky on the legs I turn because they're not straight tapers but rather swollen tapers. The wider the sandpaper you use the better.

The last thing I have to do before attaching the legs is to pop out the plug (see the bottom photo

SHAPING A LEG

1) Bandsaw out the front profile.

2) Flip the blank onto its side and cut the side profile.

3) Determine the arris.

4) Remove wood until you have a fair, smooth curve from every angle.

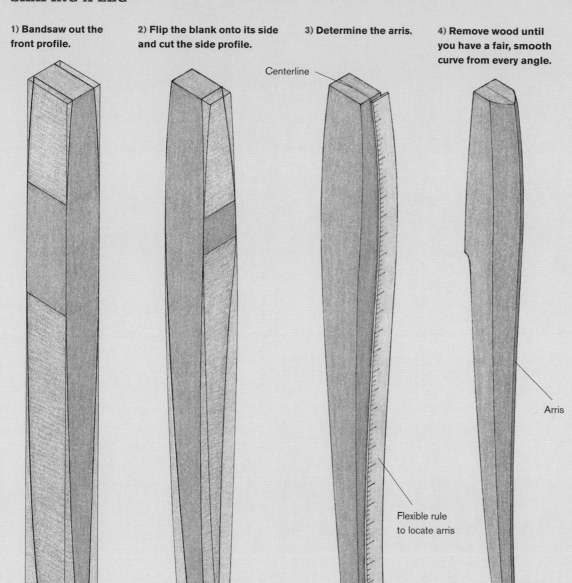

Centerline

Flexible rule to locate arris

Arris

on page 18). I just lay down the legs on a blanket on my workbench, clamp a board to the end of the bench to keep the legs from sliding off and plant my chisel where plug and pocket meet, bevel facing into the plug. A couple of sharp raps with a mallet usually will unseat the plug and then a minute of paring will clean out the pocket so that I can attach the leg to the carcase.

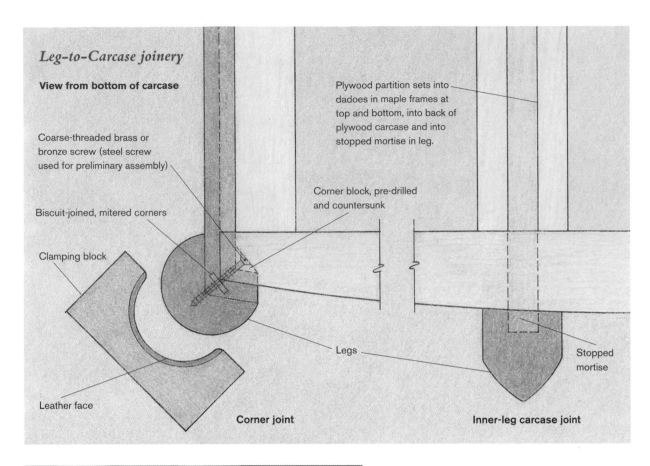

Leg-to-Carcase joinery

View from bottom of carcase

Plywood partition sets into dadoes in maple frames at top and bottom, into back of plywood carcase and into stopped mortise in leg.

Coarse-threaded brass or bronze screw (steel screw used for preliminary assembly)

Corner block, pre-drilled and countersunk

Biscuit-joined, mitered corners

Clamping block

Leather face

Legs

Corner joint

Stopped mortise

Inner-leg carcase joint

Attaching Inner Legs

When I design a relatively long piece of carcase furniture, I use six legs to distribute the weight and give the piece greater stability. Besides the four legs at the piece's corners, there are two inner legs positioned between sections of the carcase, usually between a central bank of drawers and flanking smaller sections with doors. These sections are separated inside the carcase, front to back, by a piece of hardwood plywood. This partition provides a surface to attach my web frame for the drawers in the center and to attach shelves or

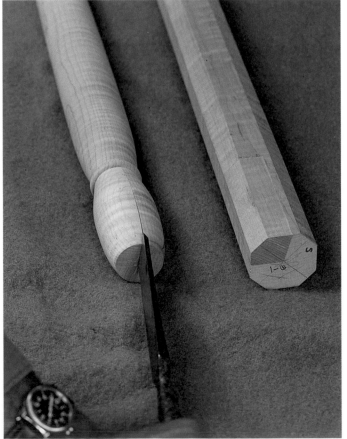

PHILBRICK REMOVES THE PLUG he spot-glued into the blank before turning the leg. A few good taps with a mallet free up the plug, which he uses to prevent tearout when turning. The blank at right was plugged while still square, and then the corners were sawn off on the tablesaw to prepare it for turning.

shelf-support hardware in the sections behind the doors. A third function of the plywood is to act as a tenon, mating with a long, stopped mortise in the back of each of the two inner legs (see the drawing on the facing page). Because there's no appreciable movement in the plywood and because the tenon is only ¾ in. thick, there's no problem with wood movement. Also, there is tremendous lateral shear strength with this joint because of the tenon's length (as long as the carcase is high) and because plywood is stronger than solid wood. I've used this joint for 27 years and never had a problem.

Attaching Legs at the Corners

The first step in attaching my legs at the corners of tables and carcase pieces depends on whether the leg is turned or shaped. The procedures I use to prepare legs are discussed on pp. 16–17. If the leg was turned, then I have to remove the wood plug I spot-glued into the blank to prevent tearout on the lathe, as shown in the photo on the facing page. If the leg was shaped, then it already has a recess or pocket in the back to mate with the corner of the apron or carcase. For tables, the aprons are mitered and splined, and for carcase pieces, I miter the mating edges and biscuit-join them.

With both tables and carcase pieces, I glue in predrilled and countersunk corner blocks. Then I dry-clamp one leg at a time, using custom-made clamping blocks (see the drawing on the facing page). With the legs clamped tightly at the corners, I drill into each leg and then screw a steel screw into the leg through the predrilled corner block, which acts as a guide for the drill bit.

Now I step back as far as I can to look at all of the legs and to make sure that they're all parallel to each other. If necessary, I'll take a block plane and shave a tad off the carcase behind where the obstinate leg will be screwed to the carcase. Just a few shavings usually does the trick.

SHAPED LEGS ALL AROUND this pau ferro hall chest give it a springiness and energy that defy its mass. The gentle cabriole-like curve of the legs is reminiscent of Queen Anne furniture but without the stiff formality.

Finally, when all legs are parallel, I back out the steel screws, glue the legs to the carcase and reclamp legs to the carcase until I can get a brass or bronze finish screw into the leg through the corner block. For a tall carcase piece, I use one full-height corner block, from the top of the carcase to the bottom, in each corner.

TIMOTHY S. PHILBRICK is a furniture maker in Narragansett, Rhode Island.

Laying Out Compound-Angle Dovetails

BY STEVE BROWN

If you can cut an accurate butt joint on a compound angle, then you can cut compound-angle dovetails. The rest is basically a layout lesson. Done well, these specialty dovetails become an attractive design element in themselves. Cradles and trays are just a few projects that require them. The drawers on a bombé-style chest are another example.

Fundamentally, compound-angle dovetails are the same as normal dovetails. The shoulders of the pins and tails are parallel to the ends of the board, and the lines for the pin faces are parallel to the top and bottom edges of the board. The angle for the flare of the tails still needs to be appropriate to the overall grain direction. And spacing the pins is still a matter of strength and individual taste. The challenge is to figure out specifically what these angles are when you factor in the compound angle, and also how to work with the awkwardly shaped boards.

By the way, with the extra angles involved, hand-cutting is probably the easiest way to form these joints. I suppose a tablesaw or bandsaw could be used, but only with a number of ramps or jigs. And as far as I can tell, a router setup simply is not possible.

HERE THE AUTHOR OFFERS **an easy layout technique that opens the door to dovetails.**

Scribe the Shoulder

The shoulder (the length of the pins and tails) is still determined by the thickness of the adjacent board. However, because these boards connect at an angle, the dimension of the shoulder line is not the actual thickness of the adjacent board but the width of its edge when cut at an angle. Sounds complicated, but all you have to do is use the angled end of one board to locate the scribe line on the other. Mark the face that has the sharper corner, because this is the edge that a marking gauge can be used on. Then carry the line across the edges using

Scribe the Shoulders and Sides of Pins

1. USE THE MARKING GAUGE on the inside face (with the sharper edge). Rub the beam along the face of the board to keep the gauge in proper alignment.

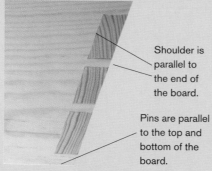

Shoulder is parallel to the end of the board.

Pins are parallel to the top and bottom of the board.

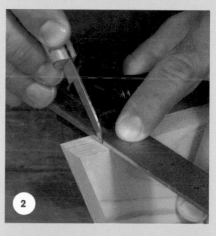

2. CARRY THE LINES ACROSS THE EDGES. Using a square with its blade laid flat along the beveled edge of the workpiece, scribe the lines with a knife.

3. CONNECT THE LINES. Last, use a straightedge and marking knife to connect the scribe lines along the outside face of the board.

4. BROWN PREFERS DOING PINS FIRST. Along the outside face of the board, mark the spacing. Set the blade of your sliding bevel gauge parallel with the top and bottom edges of the board and lay out the sides of the pins.

a square, keeping the line parallel to the beveled edge and the blade of the square flat on that edge. Last, use a straightedge to carry the shoulder line across the other face.

I prefer to cut pins before tails, but going tails–first also would be feasible here. Lay out the rise and run angles the same way to get the two bevel-gauge settings needed; then transfer those angles to the face grain of the tails boards, rather than to the end grain of the pins boards.

Rise-Run Technique Simplifies Layout

Start by laying out the pin spacing along the inside face of the board. Just as with regular dovetails, use the centerlines to mark the edges of each pin. The difference here is that the pencil lines used to lay out the sides of the pins should be parallel to the top or bottom edge of the box, not square to the end of the board.

The key point with compound-angle dovetails is that the flare of the pins (and tails) is not a single angle as it is with normal dovetails; both the direction of the grain and the centerline are parallel to the top and bottom edges of the box sides but not square to the ends of the boards. So the top and bottom of each pin are at different angles.

To find the two necessary bevel-gauge settings, set up a rise-run ratio on the face of one of the boards. To get a true 6:1

dovetail angle, don't take the rise dimensions as measurements up the face of the board. Instead, take them as elevations, with the board in its sloped position. To do this turn again to the indispensable set-up block. Lean the board against it, and then use the top face of the block and two box sides laid on top of it to make three evenly spaced marks.

Now set up the run. Draw a line through the center mark, parallel to the top and bottom edges of the box. Measure the thickness of the box sides and use that increment to make six marks along that long centerline. That's the run for a 6:1 ratio. Last, connect the sixth point with the top and bottom rise marks you made earlier. These are the correct angles for the top and bottom of each pin (or tail). Lay a sliding bevel gauge along the end of the board and take the top setting. Lay out all of the top sides of all of the pins on the box before changing the setting and laying out the other side of each pin.

Saw, Chop, and Transfer

Once the pins have been laid out, the sawing, chopping, and paring to the lines are basically the same as when making conventional dovetails, except the shapes

PROJECTS LIKE THIS SHAKER CRADLE depend on compound-angle dovetails. The angled sides make the interior more accessible.

A Rise-Run Ratio Determines the Angles

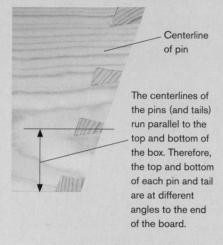

Centerline of pin

The centerlines of the pins (and tails) run parallel to the top and bottom of the box. Therefore, the top and bottom of each pin and tail are at different angles to the end of the board.

Make a Large Set-Up Block

Make it with its sides cut at the slope of the box sides. Then use the block and two of the actual box sides to lay out three equal divisions on another side of the box.

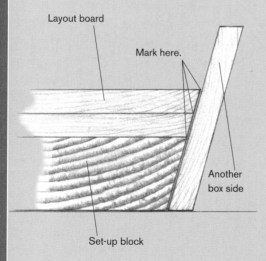

Layout board

Mark here.

Another box side

Set-up block

MARK OUT SIX DIVISIONS of the same thickness as the sides to create a 6:1 dovetail angle. Use those lines to set your sliding bevel gauge. There will be different gauge settings for the tops and bottoms of the pins.

Set the Bevel Gauge and Mark the Pins

TAKE THE TWO SETTINGS from the layout board. Lay out one of the angles on all of the pins or tails, then reset your bevel gauge to the other angle and finish the layout.

CUT THE PINS OR TAILS and transfer their locations to the mating board. It's no easy feat to keep these angled boards in perfect position during this step.

look different and might be a bit awkward to reach. You can rip an extra block while cutting the butt joint and use it as a paring block when cutting the shoulders, clamping it onto the workpiece to guide your chisel.

Transferring the layout of the pins onto the face of the tail board is similar to the regular process, but holding the boards is a bit of a challenge. Lay out the tails with a sharp pencil (a marking knife will bruise the nonwaste portion of the wood). Last, transfer the marks across the end of the board with a bevel gauge set at the appropriate angle. Don't try to mark the tails on the other side of the board. Saw, pare, and fit the tails in the standard way.

STEVE BROWN is the head of the cabinet-and furniture-making program at Boston's North Bennet Street School.

Designing the Wedged Mortise and Tenon

BY CARL SWENSSON

A door can be slammed only so many times before the tenons pull out of their mortises. Even the sturdiest chair will not survive an overweight, hyperactive teen who tilts back on the chair's rear legs. These are extremes. Most furniture that falls apart has not been abused. When a chair squeaks or a table wobbles, it's usually just bad joinery design.

Good design buys time against the use and abuse that all furniture will bear. Unless you plan to make all your furniture exclusively for your grandmother, you must choose and design furniture joints to withstand years of stress. Many antique stores offer living proof that well-made furniture can outlive its maker. Look closely at an old chair or door, and you may find the distinctive bands of wedges still holding through tenons in place.

The wedged mortise and tenon is a simply made and very effective woodworking joint (see the photo on p. 26). Two kerfs cut in the tenon accept wedges to make the tenon dovetail-shaped. To accommodate the wedged tenon, most of the mortise wall is relieved (or cut) at the same angle as the tenon wedge. This joint is particularly good at resisting racking, a common stress on table and chair legs. And as a visible and beautiful joint, it will add value beyond its structural contribution.

There are no simple guidelines to cutting a successful wedged mortise and tenon. There are no best angles or right lengths for the wedges nor any proper thicknesses for the tenon strips. Designing the wedged mortise and tenon must take into account not only the many stresses the finished piece must withstand but also the particular characteristics of the wood, even of the particular boards you use. The design process must leave the drawing table and become part of the construction process.

The Stresses that Break Joints

There are two types of forces that work joints loose: internal, from the seasonal expansion and contraction of the wood, and external, from human use. Unless you live in an environment with perfectly controlled humidity, variations in the wood's moisture content are inevitable. Because of the cross-grain construction in joints like a mortise and tenon, these seasonal changes are a long-term threat to the joint's integrity. Quartersawn lumber

SWENSSON TAPS
IN WEDGES that
won't come out.
Careful design will
yield a joint that is
nearly impossible
to pull apart.

The Wedged Mortise and Tenon

A cutaway view of a well-proportioned joint shows all parts fitting snugly. Wedges tapped into sawkerfs in the tenon clamp the tenon strips against the mortise walls. The dovetail-shaped tenon will not withdraw from the mortise under tension, but joint integrity depends mainly on the strength of the tenon strips.

Wedge   Tenon   Tenon strip

Tenon member

Mortise member

Wedge

Strip thickness between 3/32 in. and 3/16 in.

Area of mortise relief

Sawkerf in tenon

Leave from one-quarter to one-fifth of the mortise wall unrelieved.

1/8 in.

Ideally, the wedge should extend at least 1/8 in. past relief cut, with a 1/8-in. space at bottom of kerf.

Angle between 1:10 and 1:5

is more stable than flatsawn and should be used for all joints. This grain orientation ensures that the wood will move the least along its greatest width. It also minimizes the wood's movement against itself.

Normal use will put several forces on a joint: compression and tension, shearing, racking, and twisting. The connection between the internal faces of the mortise and tenon does most of the work in keeping the joint together, though the tenon's shoulders help to prevent compression.

Twisting forces are often overlooked in joint design. Kicking a table leg or leaning back on the rear legs of a chair can create very strong twisting forces on a joint. A mortise near the end of a board is particularly vulnerable to this stress because of the

short grain. It is better to keep the mortise at least twice the width of the tenon away from the end of the board. These forces will be less likely to cause joint failure.

Wedging the Tenon Against Tension

A simple glued mortise-and-tenon joint with shoulders will resist compression, shearing, racking, and twisting forces quite well. But this joint does not respond well to tension. In time, when the glue crumbles away, the tenon will come out almost as easily as it went in.

Wedging the tenon creates an internal dovetail shape that is extremely resistant to tension and does not compromise the joint's strength in any other way (see the

Strip Thickness

TEST TENON STRIP MATERIAL WITH A TEMPLATE. A few outside fibers have failed on this test strip, but it is basically sound.

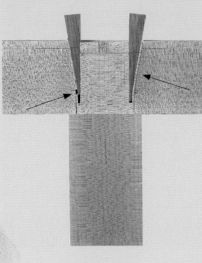

STRIPS ARE TOO THIN. A little tension on the joint has broken one of the strips and allowed the tenon to withdraw. The layout line at the top shows how the parts have moved.

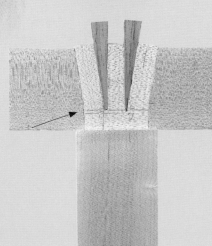

STRIPS ARE TOO THICK. Even though they were tough, the tenon strips were asked to deflect too much and have cracked substantially at the base. Note how the layout lines at the bottom have moved.

drawing on p. 27). Under tension, the mortise walls exert an even clamping pressure along the side of the tenon. This pressure holds the wedges firmly inside the tenon and does not squeeze them out of their kerfs. As long as the tenon keeps its dovetail shape, it will not withdraw under either tension pressure.

The key to the strength of this joint is the integrity of the thin strip of tenon between the wedge and the mortise wall. The joint is nearly impossible to break under tension if the strip remains intact. However, if both strips break, the tenon will not resist withdrawal any more than a plain tenon would. The variables affecting the soundness of the tenon strip are its thickness, the mortise-relief angle, the length of the mortise-relief angle, and the length of the kerf in the tenon. Each of these must be determined in turn. As the examples on this and the facing page show, it's easy to misjudge one of these factors.

Templates to Test Thicknesses and Angles

Determining the tenon-strip thickness and mortise-relief angle as a working unit depends largely on the properties of the wood you are using. Hard maple will often work in a wide range of thicknesses and angles. More brittle woods, such as cherry, may require a very low angle ratio and a thin strip to work. Even variations from board to board make it necessary to test the angle and strip for each project.

Make a series of templates with slope ratios from 1:10 to 1:5 to simulate the mortise-relief angles in the actual joint (see the top photo at left). File or chisel a slight round at the angle, both on the test jig and in the actual joint. This reduces the chances that the tenon strip will kink, crack or break when it bends around the angle. Next make five to six strips of various thicknesses from the same wood as the tenon, preferably from the same board. I recommend making them not less than ³⁄₃₂ in. and not more than ³⁄₁₆ in.

Clamp the strips to the different templates until you find the combination of greatest thickness and highest angle that will not break the strip. A higher angle gives better withdrawal resistance, but requires a thinner and more vulnerable strip (see the center photo on the facing page). A lower angle can accommodate a thicker strip, which is less likely to break, but will not offer as much resistance to tension. However, really thick strips do not bend as easily and may crack if bent too far (see the bottom photo on the facing page). As a rule, I start testing with a strip ³⁄₃₂ in. thick and a slope ratio of 1:7 and increase either the ratio or the thickness or both from there to find the best balance.

Proportions for Mortise Wall Relief and Tenon Kerf

You now know the angle to relieve the mortise wall and to cut the wedges. The next step is to determine how much of the mortise wall you should relieve. This will, in turn, determine the length of the wedge and the depth of the kerf in the tenon.

The deeper the mortise-relief cut is, the more surface area you create on the mortise wall to resist tension. However, you must leave some room at the base of the tenon so the wedge can be driven past the end of the mortise relief. Leaving from one-quarter to one-fifth of the mortise wall unrelieved works well.

The sawkerf in the tenon should extend beyond the mortise-relief cut, but not by much. This allows the wedge to be driven farther than the end of the mortise relief without bottoming out in the kerf. That ensures the tenon strip will be pressed snugly against the entire relieved mortise wall. Driving the wedge beyond the relief cut also allows the wedge to support the

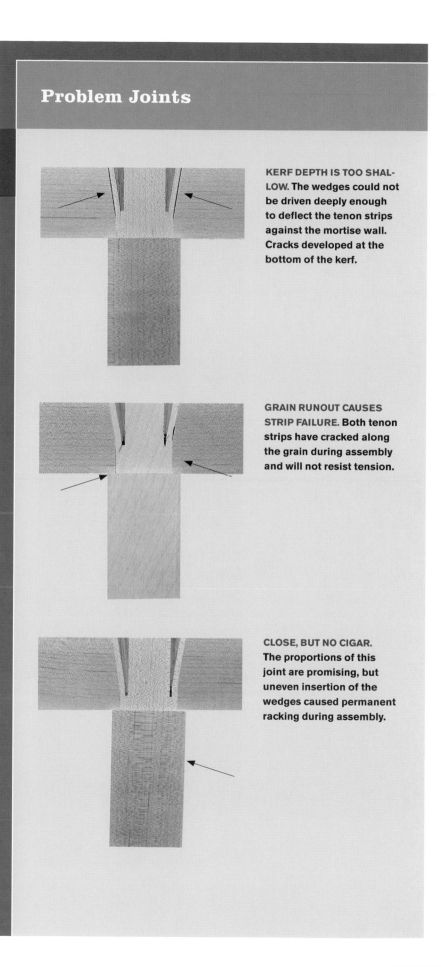

Problem Joints

KERF DEPTH IS TOO SHALLOW. The wedges could not be driven deeply enough to deflect the tenon strips against the mortise wall. Cracks developed at the bottom of the kerf.

GRAIN RUNOUT CAUSES STRIP FAILURE. Both tenon strips have cracked along the grain during assembly and will not resist tension.

CLOSE, BUT NO CIGAR. The proportions of this joint are promising, but uneven insertion of the wedges caused permanent racking during assembly.

weakest side of the strip where it bends. If the kerf is too shallow, the wedge will bottom out, and the strip cannot be compressed against the mortise wall (see the top photo on p. 29). Trying to insert the wedges farther during assembly may cause a split in the tenon.

If the tenon has grain runout, splits that develop during assembly may follow the grain out of the wood, causing complete joint failure (see the center photo on p. 29). The first defense against such splits is selecting straight-grained wood for the tenon member. Deep sawkerfs and the snug fit of all the parts in the joint also will help prevent this problem.

Another way to keep a strip from splitting is to drill a ⅛-in.-dia. relief hole at the bottom of the kerf. It will distribute the stress at this point. The hole also thins the strip where it bends, helping it to take the bend without cracking. This step should not be necessary if the grain is straight and the relief angle and strip thickness are well-balanced.

The Wedges for Final Assembly

Perhaps, without realizing it, you have already designed the wedges. The angle of the wedges is the same as the slope ratio of the mortise relief. The thickness of the wedges at their tip should be a little less than the tenon kerf. The wedges should be at least ⅜ in. longer than the kerf is deep to make it easier to tap in during assembly.

Final assembly, however, is not the time to relax. Much of the joint's integrity depends on how well the parts come together. If you hammer the wedges in unevenly, the joint will rack to one side (see the bottom photo on p. 29). Keep the joint square and the tenon firmly in the mortise as you tap in the wedges.

Yellow wood glue, because it sets fast, can make this joint even trickier to assemble. It sets so fast you won't have much time to make sure all the parts are aligned properly.

For this joint, I use a glue with a slower set-up time. If you have avoided design mistakes, the result should be a very tight, strong joint and an ornament to your work.

CARL SWENSSON is a professional woodworker and furniture designer. He has built tracker organs, doors for a Buddhist temple in Japan, and countless Appalachian-style chairs. He lives in Baltimore, Maryland.

Compound Angles
without Math

BY STEVE BROWN

Compound angles add visual interest to a piece. Instead of building a cradle that looks like a stiff box, you can angle the sides to give it a more subtle, inviting appearance. Angled sides are used in many types of woodwork, from simple serving trays and window boxes to the high-style bombé chest, with its flat, sloped case and drawers that are carved into a bulge on the outside.

A compound angle occurs at the intersection of two sloped sides, and there are a number of joints that can be used to connect them. The most basic and fundamental of these is the butt joint. Miter joints and dovetails are more complex options. At North Bennet Street School, where I teach, we've found an easy tablesaw method that handles all three variations required, with some handwork for dovetails.

WORK FROM A MODEL. By beveling the edges of a wood block at the desired slope for your sides, you create a working model of the box or tray and all of its angles. Used alone, laid on its side, the block gives you the blade and miter-gauge angles for a butt joint; add a 45° triangle (right), and you have the settings for a miter.

Pick a Slope, Any Slope

To make the set-up block, you need to know only the slope of the sides of the box. Set the sawblade to that angle and bevel three edges of a long block. The block becomes a working model of the box and all of its angles can be used to set up the tablesaw to cut the joints.

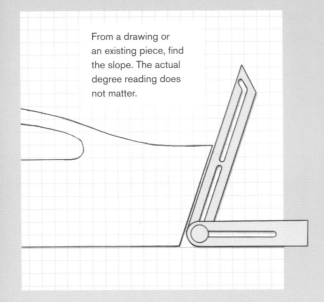

From a drawing or an existing piece, find the slope. The actual degree reading does not matter.

TRANSFER THAT ANGLE TO THE BLADE. This is a good time to rip the top and bottom edges of the box sides, which usually are cut at this angle.

To form a compound angle on the tablesaw, both the blade and the miter gauge must be angled for crosscutting. The problem is that you cannot get those angle settings from the standard views on drawings. When any piece features surfaces that are not perpendicular to the line of sight, there is distortion in their size and shape. Take the front side of a simple box. If each side slopes outward 10 degrees, the front and side views will show a slightly shortened front side, and the crosscut angle at each end will be distorted. The top view is also deceiving—you are not looking straight down on the top edges of the box, so you can't read the true bevel angle of the butt joints.

There are a few traditional approaches to calculating these two angle settings. The first involves drafting a corrected view that shows the true dimensions and angles of each side of the box. The second is a mathematical solution using trigonometry. However, while working through these traditional solutions with our students, we became dissatisfied with their complexity and potential for inaccuracy. There are chances for error when drawing or making calculations and also when you turn those numbers into actual tablesaw settings. This led us to rethink the problem and eventually figure out a simpler method for determining and cutting compound angles on the tablesaw.

A Set-Up Block Is a Simple Solution

To carry out this method, you need to know only the slope angle for the sides. This slope is also usually the blade angle used to rip the top and bottom edges of each side. If the slope is 10 degrees, for

NOW MAKE THE SET-UP BLOCK. Mill a flat, square block roughly 2 in. thick by 3 in. wide by 10 in. long. Then rip one edge (left) and crosscut the two ends at the slope angle (above).

example, most designs call for a 10 degree bevel along the top and bottom edges.

The basic trick is using that same blade angle to bevel the edges of a set-up block, which then becomes a working model of the box and all of its angles (see the photos and drawing above and on the facing page). That's it. The edges of the block represent the sides of the box. Simply flip the block on one edge and slide an adjacent edge against the blade to find the appropriate blade and crosscut angles for an accurate butt joint.

This approach lets you walk up to the saw with any slope in mind and quickly create tight joints. Start by ripping the box parts to width (or height, depending on your perspective) with the appropriate bevel on the top and bottom edges. Next, joint and plane a block of wood flat and square on all sides. Make the block roughly

2 in. thick by at least 3 in. wide by 10 in. long, for reasons that will become apparent later. Next, crosscut each end of the block and rip at least one side at the same blade angle you used to bevel the sides. If necessary, you can hold the box parts in place against the block to see if the slope suits your tastes. You now have your set-up block.

Cut the Basic Butt Joint

At this point a butt joint is easy to produce. Set the blade angle first. Lay the block on one of its beveled sides and change the blade angle until it is flush with the angled end of the block (the block should be narrow enough to fit against the side of the blade without hitting the teeth). Next, keeping the block on its side, hold it against the miter-gauge fence. Adjust the miter-gauge angle until the end of the block

Compound-Angle Butt Joint

The set-up block is all you need to cut a perfect compound-angle butt joint. The block should be narrow enough to fit under the teeth of the blade when it is fully raised, with the end of the block flush against the blade's side.

1. USE THE BLOCK TO SET THE BLADE AND MITER-GAUGE ANGLES

Set-up block

Place long beveled face down.

FIND BOTH ANGLES IN ONE STEP. Place the set-up block on its long beveled side. Pivot it forward and back while changing the blade angle until the end of the block is flush against the blade.

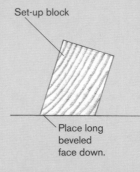

HOLD THE BLOCK IN PLACE and bring up the miter gauge. When the gauge is flush to the block, lock in the angle setting.

mates perfectly with the flat face of the blade. The saw is now set up to cut the correct compound angle on all of the sides.

Tablesaws tilt only one way, so one end of each side will be crosscut on the left side of the blade, with the miter gauge riding in the left miter slot. The other end will be cut on the other side of the blade, with the board flipped edge for edge onto its other face. To help keep track of the cuts, lay out each one and label the inside and outside faces of each part before starting.

This simple approach usually yields a perfectly fitting joint on the first try; however, just to be safe, I recommend cutting a sample joint first. Then set the parts against the set-up block to check the joint. If any adjustments to the miter fence or blade angle are necessary, take another slice off the sample sides and check the joint again. Remember to save all of your offcuts; you'll be able to use them as clamping blocks later during glue-up.

2. CUT BOTH ENDS OF THE BOARD

SWITCH MITER SLOTS, NOT SETTINGS.
There's no need to change the blade angle when cutting opposite ends of a box side; just flip the board edge for edge and move the miter gauge to the other side of the blade. Label the inside and outside faces of each part and lay out all of the cuts to keep track of them. Also, use a stop block to index the second cut on each side.

Miters Aren't Much Harder

To cut miters, the crosscut angle stays the same; only the blade angle has to change. To find that new angle, you will need a 45 degree triangle. When you have the set-up block on its side and the miter fence properly angled, lay the triangle against the top face of the set-up block. Now crank the blade angle over until it mates with the edge of the triangle (see the left photo on p. 36).

What is happening here is complex mathematically but much simpler

visually. If you look at the top view of the box with butt joints, the sides will appear to meet at a 90 degree angle. Although you know that the ends of the boards were not crosscut with the blade at 90 degrees, from that angle (looking straight down on the sloped sides), the joint is square. That's why you can lay a square across the beveled top edge of the set-up block or the box itself and find a 90 degree angle between the sides. Likewise, a miter on this compound-angle joint will actually be 45 degrees when viewed from the top. By placing the

Compound Angle Miter Joint

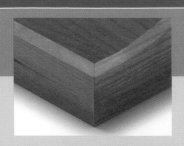

To turn the butt joint into a miter joint, simply add a 45° triangle to the front face of the set-up block and reset the blade angle. The miter-gauge angle stays at the butt-joint setting.

PLACE THE TRIANGLE FLAT against the front face of the set-up block. Angle the blade to meet the edge of the triangle.

AGAIN, LAY OUT AND LABEL the sides to keep track of the cuts. Workpiece creep is especially a problem with these sharply angled cuts, so clamp on a stop block, or a stop stick.

MITER-JOINT CLAMPING STRATEGY. Rip some scrap stock at the current blade angle and glue these blocks onto the workpieces. Use these clamping cauls to draw the joint tightly together. The blocks can be pared away later.

triangle flat across the top side of the set-up block, you are using this phenomenon to find the right blade angle for a perfect miter. The blade will not actually be 45 degrees from the table, of course, because the triangle itself is being held at an angle. If all of this doesn't make perfect sense to you, don't worry; the procedure will work anyway.

With this technique you'll never have to fear compound angles. You can cut a butt or miter joint at any angle. You can even set adjacent sides of a box at different angles and still determine the tablesaw settings for perfect joints. Also, with the butt joint in your repertoire, dovetails are just a layout procedure away.

STEVE BROWN is the head of the cabinet-and furniture-making program at North Bennet Street School in Boston, Massachusetts.

Simplified Three-Way Miter

BY RICHARD J. GOTZ

1. Cut mortises while the stock is square.

2. Miter the members on the two inside faces.

3. Assemble the parts using plywood loose tenons that are beveled on two edges.

ANATOMY OF A THREE-WAY MITER JOINT. A simplified version of the three-way miter uses loose tenons to join the members. The material must be dimensioned perfectly square, and the mortises and miters must be cut exactly the same on each piece for the joint to fit together cleanly.

The three-way miter is a deceptively simple-looking joint on the outside. Three equally dimensioned pieces of wood join at a corner with miters showing on three faces. One primary reason for its aesthetic appeal is that only long grain is visible; the end grain is hidden where the pieces join. While simple-looking from the outside, when constructed with traditional methods, the three-way miter is anything but simple on the inside.

Complex forms of the joint, which date back to Ming dynasty furniture making, require precision cuts with hand tools. Some methods of constructing the three-way miter utilize hidden dovetails, sliding dovetails, or quadruple tenons. Because of this, the three-way miter is not often used by the amateur craftsperson. But it needn't be so daunting. Although there probably are a dozen or more ways to cut a three-way miter, I use a method that is straightforward and relies on only a few cuts with power tools.

Use This Method for Light-Duty Furniture

After attending a few weekend classes with Toshio Odate and Yeung Chan, I was inspired to create a piece of Asian-style furniture that would incorporate some of the design details they suggested. I came upon the three-way miter joint, but I was overwhelmed with the elaborate techniques involved. Just in drawing the traditional method of construction, the joint was a humbling experience; I could only imagine

how difficult it would be to cut it with a handsaw and chisel.

I decided to forgo the most elaborate forms of the three-way miter for a modern method. I tried a couple described in books by Chan and Gary Rogowski, but they required several different settings on the tablesaw, with each pass needing readjustment of the miter gauge, fence, or blade height. It was clear that achieving a tight fit with either method was going to require great precision in my setup. Any inaccuracy multiplies with subsequent readjustments and cuts.

To reduce the chance of inaccuracy, I decided it would be necessary to reduce the number of individual cuts. I landed on a

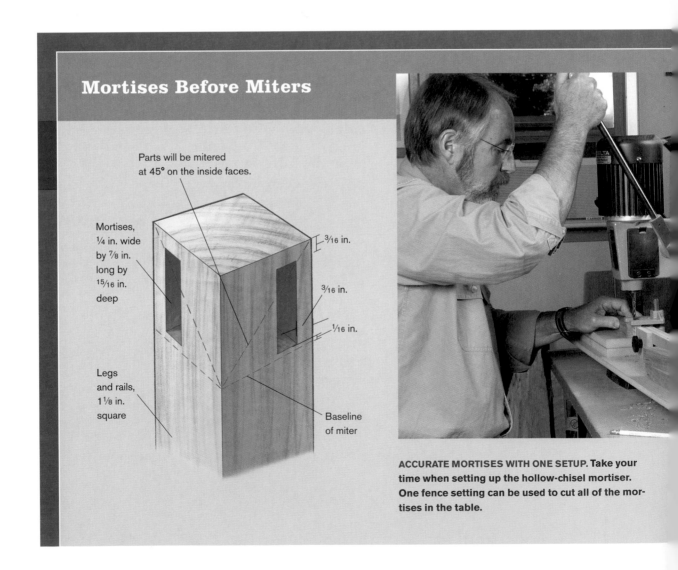

Mortises Before Miters

Parts will be mitered at 45° on the inside faces.

Mortises, ¼ in. wide by ⅞ in. long by ¹⁵⁄₁₆ in. deep

³⁄₁₆ in.

³⁄₁₆ in.

¹⁄₁₆ in.

Legs and rails, 1⅛ in. square

Baseline of miter

ACCURATE MORTISES WITH ONE SETUP. Take your time when setting up the hollow-chisel mortiser. One fence setting can be used to cut all of the mortises in the table.

method in which all of the mortises are cut with one fence setting on a hollow-chisel mortiser; all of the miters are cut with one setting on the tablesaw; and loose tenons are used to join the pieces. Furthermore, the four rails and four legs that make up the basic table are all produced with the same series of cuts.

The strength of the three-way miter using this method, for the most part, relies on the loose tenons. Because the mitered surfaces of the rails and legs may not provide an adequate bond, be careful how you plan to use this joint. I would recommend it for light-duty use only. Aprons or stretchers will increase the strength, as will larger tenons.

Legs and Rails Must Be Equal in Width and Thickness

Depending on the project you take on, your material can be any thickness and length. But for the basic table pictured in this article, I chose to make the legs and rails 1⅛ in. square. Starting with 6/4 lumber, mill the rough stock to size with a jointer, planer, and tablesaw. The thickness and width of each piece must be equal for the joint to assemble correctly, so my final step was to run each piece through the planer on its face and edge.

When you finish dimensioning each piece, you should have four equally sized

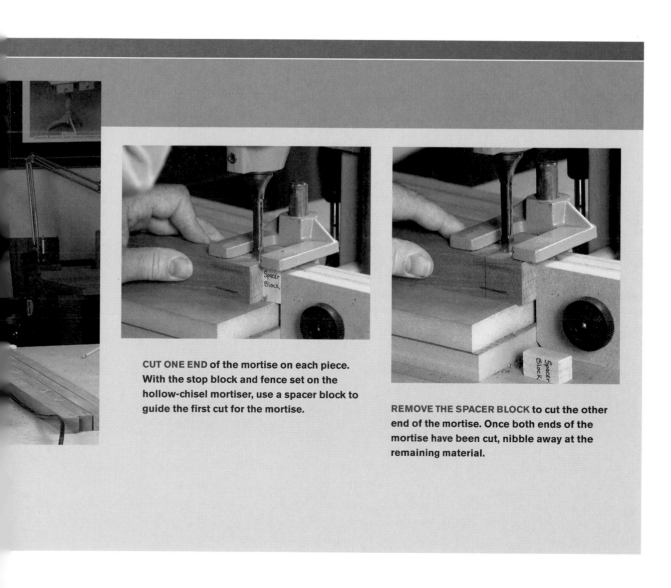

CUT ONE END of the mortise on each piece. With the stop block and fence set on the hollow-chisel mortiser, use a spacer block to guide the first cut for the mortise.

REMOVE THE SPACER BLOCK to cut the other end of the mortise. Once both ends of the mortise have been cut, nibble away at the remaining material.

Miters Must Be Accurate

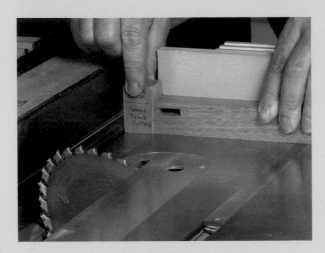

BUTT THE WORKPIECE against a stop block. Position the stop block so that the sawblade cuts right to the corner of the workpiece. Be sure you don't cut past the corner line. The first miter is cut with the workpiece held so that one mortise is facing the blade and the other is facing the surface of the tablesaw.

legs and four rails. One pair of rails determines the table width; the other pair determines the table depth.

All of the Mortises Are Identical

On the end of each leg where it meets the rails, cut two adjacent mortises. In addition, each rail will have two adjacent mortises cut at both ends. I used a hollow-chisel mortiser for this operation. However, if you don't have a hollow-chisel mortiser, you can rough-cut the mortises with a drill press and carve them clean with a chisel.

Set up the hollow-chisel mortiser with a ¼-in. bit so that it cuts ³⁄₁₆ in. from the fence. You can set the fence-to-bit distance by holding a ³⁄₁₆-in. drill bit in between. Cut the adjacent mortises with the out-

side faces of the legs and rails registered off the fence. This will require that half of the mortises be cut with the material sticking out to the left of the bit and half with the material sticking out to the right. For each orientation (left facing and right facing), set a stop block ³⁄₁₆ in. from the bit to cut one end of the mortise. A spacer block is used to set up the cut in the other end of the mortise. The spacer block is equal to the length of the mortise (⅞ in.), less the width of the hollow chisel. Once both ends of the mortise have been cut, remove the remaining material in between.

At this point, you can use a smoothing plane to remove any marks on the surfaces of the legs and rails. It's best to do this before you cut the miters so as not to damage the fragile corners.

ROTATE THE WORKPIECE to cut the adjacent miter. The mortise that was facing the surface of the tablesaw should be facing the miter gauge on the second cut.

Precise Miters Create a Tight-Fitting Joint

For the four mitered corners of the table to be assembled absolutely square, it is paramount that you cut the miters exactly 45 degrees—no more, no less. I chose to cut the miters with a miter gauge set at 90 degrees and the tablesaw blade at 45 degrees.

Make practice cuts with scrapwood before cutting into your project material. To test for square, cut two miters, place them together, and measure the 90 degree angle with an accurate square. If there is any discernible gap, adjust your sawblade and try again.

The miters are cut on each face where you already have cut the mortises. That

means the legs will have two adjacent mitered sides, and the rails will have four miters (two on each end).

When cutting the adjacent miters, make the first cut with the material positioned so that one mortise is facing the surface of the tablesaw and one mortise is facing the blade. To cut the adjacent miter, rotate the workpiece forward so that the mortise that was facing the surface of the tablesaw is now facing the fence of the miter gauge. Beware of flying debris produced by this second cut. The small, pyramid-shaped cut-off has a tendency to ricochet off the blade unless you pass the material slowly across it.

Once both miters have been cut, flip the workpiece and make the same two cuts on the opposite end. Always use a stop block to

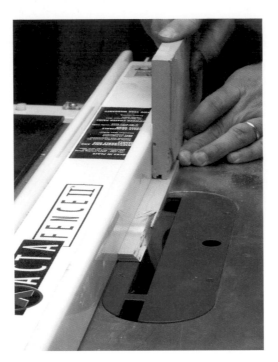

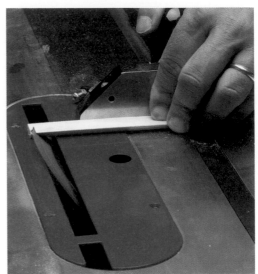

CUT THE TENONS from a long strip of material. Cut a bevel along one edge of the tenon stock. Then bevel one end and crosscut to length.

position the workpiece for each cut. I also glue 180-grit sandpaper to the face of the miter gauge to prevent the workpiece from slipping.

Mitered Loose Tenons Increase the Gluing Surface

To produce a stable and strong joint, I make loose tenons from Baltic birch plywood. I increase the gluing surface of the tenons by mitering two of their edges.

Starting with ½-in.-thick plywood, rip several 12-in.-long pieces at ⅞ in. wide. Next, bring them down to the thickness of the mortises so that they fit just right—not too tight and not too loose. You can do this on a tablesaw or planer. It's a good idea to cut these strips ahead of time because the subsequent cuts are made with the tablesaw blade set to 45 degrees. Because you just cut the miters at that angle, you don't have to reset the sawblade.

Cut one edge of the plywood strip to 45 degrees. Then crosscut each end of the strip with the blade still at 45 degrees. With both ends mitered, cut one tenon from each end of the strip on a radial-arm

saw or miter saw. Continue the process of mitering the ends and then chopping them to size until all 12 tenons have been cut. Cutting small pieces with power tools generally is a dangerous process, so use extreme caution.

After the tenons have been cut, arrange all of the legs and rails in the same orientation. Glue one tenon into each end of the rails and one tenon into the mitered end of the legs, making sure that the tenons are fully seated in the mortises. If not, they will prevent the joint from closing all the way. Also, all of the tenons should be glued into corresponding mortises. I chose to glue them into the mortise on the right side as I'm looking at the two mortises straight on.

Assembly Requires Two Stages

Before gluing up the table, verify that the four legs and four rails are ready and oriented correctly. If you plan to incorporate aprons into the design, have them ready as well. Mark all of the pieces, then dry-fit them together. Once you are satisfied with the dry-fit, proceed with the glue-up.

Four Steps to Assembly

BEGIN BY GLUING ONE TENON into each of the mitered ends (1). Gotz chose the mortise on the right. Then, using a frame clamp, glue one full side of the table (2). Fit a spacer block at the foot of the table to prevent the legs from bowing inward during glue-up. Fit the two remaining rails into the joint (3). If the tenons fit tightly, this may require moderate force. Finally, clamp the table for final glue-up (4). If necessary, use spacer blocks on the foot end of the table to prevent the legs from bowing.

Glue up two full sides of the table separately, let them set, and then join the two sides by gluing the two final rails in place. I use a frame clamp to glue one full side with a spacer set between the bottom of the legs to prevent them from bowing inward.

It would be nice if the clamps were transparent to detect any gaps in the miters,

but you'll have to trust the part of the joint that is visible. If you have carefully cut the miters to 45 degrees and aligned the mortises, the actual glue-up should go without incident.

RICHARD J. GOTZ is a software engineer and woodworker in Plymouth, Minnesota.

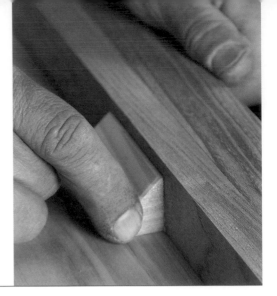

Fortify Your Joinery

BY GARRETT HACK

Repairing furniture has taught me many lessons about what joints, woods, and techniques survive decades of use. One technique I see often in well-made work is the use of corner blocks to strengthen connections or hold parts in position. Often you'll find these small blocks glued behind bracket feet and crown moldings or under drawer bottoms and chair seats.

Corner blocks are simple, but for them to be effective, it's important to choose the right wood, use the right glue, orient the grain direction appropriately, and allow for wood movement.

White pine, poplar, and basswood are my first choices for most corner blocks because they shape easily and provide adequate strength. For chairs, I prefer cherry, walnut, or mahogany blocks, which are harder woods but still can be fitted easily with planes and chisels. With the exception of an occasional brad or screw to hold a block in position, corner blocks planed to fit can be glued into place using a rub joint. Apply glue and rub the block back and forth until the glue grabs, holding the block in place—there's no need for clamps. I use yellow glue because it is strong, grabs quickly, and allows a tiny bit of creep or movement. I try to orient the grain of the block in the same direction as the grain of the wood to which it's attached, but sometimes one face of the block will be joined across the grain. In these cases, glue with a little flexibility is useful.

I think of corner blocks as points of strength, spaced apart from each other in much the same way as I use screws or nails. The short length of corner blocks, between 2 in. and 3 in., makes them easy to fit, especially when shaped into curved places. More important, compared with screws or nails, short blocks are less affected by wood movement in the piece to which they're attached.

Blocks Reinforce Case-Work Joinery

Typical case-work construction is full of joints and other places suitable for corner blocks. I have seen case tops secured by corner blocks alone that are still holding after a century or longer. While I wouldn't use corner blocks in this manner (too much potential wood movement on all but the smallest tops), they are ideal for reinforcing bracket feet, the knees of cabriole legs, or the connection of the base to the case.

Attractive bracket feet often are mitered at the corners with the grain running horizontally, making for a weak joint. Vertical

Two Ways to Strengthen Bracket Feet

Corner blocks for bracket feet can be made of white pine, poplar, or basswood. The grain of bracket feet generally runs horizontally, and the grain of corner blocks can run either vertically or horizontally.

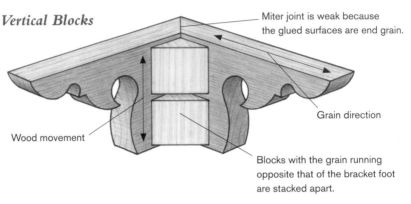

Vertical Blocks

Miter joint is weak because the glued surfaces are end grain.

Grain direction

Wood movement

Blocks with the grain running opposite that of the bracket foot are stacked apart.

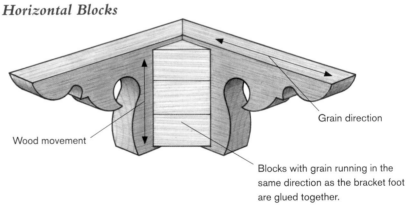

Horizontal Blocks

Grain direction

Wood movement

Blocks with grain running in the same direction as the bracket foot are glued together.

grain legs, as in the butternut chest on p. 45, are only slightly stronger because the glue surfaces of the miters are long grain.

Corner blocks behind a bracket foot can run horizontally with the grain of the foot or vertically against it (see the drawings above). Run horizontally, the blocks can be stacked and glued together so they shrink and swell along with the foot; however, the glued surfaces are weak short grain. Run vertically, the blocks are strong because the glued surfaces are long grain. But you need to keep the blocks short and spaced apart so that each can move as the foot shrinks and swells. I tend to run blocks vertically because they are easier to fit.

Corner blocks also can strengthen the connection of base to case, or bottom to case sides (see p. 44). Where the sides and bottom meet and the corner blocks

Short Blocks Support Moldings at the Top of a Casepiece

Corner blocks strengthen the joinery between the case and large moldings. Blocks at the front of the case are glued to the case and molding; at the rear of the sides, they are glued only to the molding and secured with screws in slotted holes to allow for movement.

Projecting molding

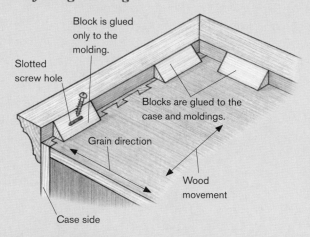

Block is glued only to the molding.

Slotted screw hole

Blocks are glued to the case and moldings.

Grain direction

Wood movement

Case side

Cantilevered molding

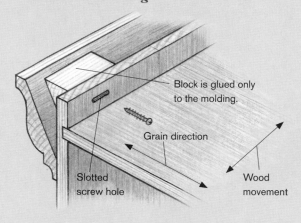

Block is glued only to the molding.

Grain direction

Slotted screw hole

Wood movement

Small Blocks
Brace Drawer Bottoms

Corner blocks can be glued to the underside of drawers to provide rigidity to the sides and to keep the bottom secure in its groove.

run cross-grain, the blocks must be short enough, about 2 in., to stay attached as the wood under them shrinks or swells.

Blocks Are Used to Attach Molding

When designing crown molding for a cabinet, I often include a bead or a similar detail to hide the brads used to attach the molding. However, brads alone are not sufficient support for a large molding, or even a smaller one, that projects above the carcase top. Corner blocks are an ideal way to strengthen this connection as well as any joints in the molding.

Run the grain of the blocks in the same direction as the molding. Grain movement is a concern only along the sides of very deep cases, where the molding runs cross-grain. Instead of gluing blocks to the case

top, use screws in slotted holes, and glue only the joint between the blocks and the molding (see the drawings on p. 47).

To avoid wasting expensive, thick stock, crown molding often is cut out of a board or built up of separate parts and therefore must be angled (or cantilevered) away from the case. Corner blocks, cut to fit between case and molding, help secure the molding at the proper angle and greatly strengthen the connection.

Blocks Stabilize Deep, Narrow Drawers

A well-engineered drawer shouldn't need corner blocks, although I have seen the underside of drawers with many blocks stuck between sides and bottom and between drawer face and bottom. In these cases, the drawer sides and face were quite thin, and the groove holding the bottom was too shallow or worn to hold it securely.

On small drawers, especially deep, narrow ones with thin sides that can flex in or out slightly, the addition of a few tiny corner blocks under the bottom and against the sides will make the drawer more rigid and keep the bottom from popping out. Place the blocks near the middle of the drawer sides so the bottom can move slightly forward and back from them. Another option is to place the blocks between the drawer face and bottom to keep them well engaged and to direct any movement of the drawer bottom to the back only. Orient the grain of the blocks in the same direction as the sides or face of the drawer they're glued to.

Blocks Strengthen Hardworking Chair Joints

Corner blocks add measurably to the strength of a chair. Not only do they make the seat more rigid and help support the

Thick Blocks Reinforce Chair Rails

Made of cherry, walnut, or mahogany, corner blocks add considerable strength to a chair. These blocks generally are glued and screwed into place (right).

FITTING A BLOCK TO CURVED RAILS. Slip a piece of carbon paper between the block and the rail, and shift the block slightly to mark any high spots (above left). Then remove those spots with a block plane (left).

seat frame, but they also strengthen the vital leg-to-rail joints.

Fit and secure the corner blocks individually after the chair has been glued. For strength, make each block as thick as possible and about 5 in. long, with the grain running horizontally and parallel with the length of the block (see the photos above). Positioned at roughly 45 degrees across the joint, a block ideally fills an entire corner, tying adjacent seat rails to each other and butting against the leg.

Fitting is a process of trial and error; first plane one side of the block for a tight fit and then the other. For maximum strength, glue the block in place and drive one or two screws through it into each seat rail.

The use of hidden corner blocks is a simple technique for adding considerable strength to certain joints. I use them anytime they fit the need.

GARRETT HACK is a contributing editor to *Fine Woodworking* magazine.

Through Mortise-and-Tenon Joinery

BY JIM RICHEY

It's hard to hide mistakes in through mortise-and-tenon joints. Both the tenon and the mortise are there for anyone to see. I found it tough to get crisp, chip-free mortises that were uniform and had clean, square corners. Then, not too long ago, I came across a drawing of a simple bench made from 1x12 stock, like the one shown in the photo at left. I wanted to build several of them, but the joint that held the bench together was a wedged through mortise and tenon. The bench was an incentive. I worked on my technique and experimented with prototypes until I could cut this joint quickly and accurately.

In a through mortise and tenon, the tenon goes all the way through its mating piece and shows on the other side. Wedges are often added to spread the end of the tenon and lock the joint together. It's a strong, attractive joint.

I can cut the mortises by hand, but when I'm faced with making a lot of them, I like to use a machine. In my shop, that means using either the drill press or the router. I prefer using the drill press because it's quiet and setup is fast and accurate.

WORK CAREFULLY when joinery is exposed. The author cuts mortises first and then marks the tenons to reduce tearout on the face side.

When I'm boring holes for a through mortise, I try to minimize tearout where the bit exits the stock. If possible, I'll select the side where tearout will be the least noticeable; then I'll lay out and cut the mortise from the opposite side. If tearout is unacceptable on either side, then I'll use a router and a jig. For this bench, though, I decided I could live with some minor tearout on the back side because this area is fairly well hidden.

Cut the Mortises First

The usual approach is to build from the "inside out." That is, cut the tenons first, and then use the tenons as a template to mark the mortise locations. The problem is that you drill the mortises from the back, which virtually guarantees some tearout on the face of the piece, no matter how careful you are. I prefer the "outside-in" approach—cut the mortises first by drilling from the face side, and then mark the tenon locations from the mortises.

To do it this way, I set up my drill press with a Forstner® bit and a fence to register the workpiece (see step 1 of the drawings above). Forstner bits are best for this operation because they make such clean cuts. Just remember that the bit diameter should be equal to or slightly smaller than the tenon thickness. You can always enlarge a mortise that's too narrow.

To minimize tearout, I set the drill-press depth stop so that the bit just goes through the workpiece or leaves a paper-thin layer of material on the bottom of the mortise. It's best to back up the workpiece with a clean piece of scrap.

I drill the first hole at one end of the mortise. Then I nibble away the remaining waste by sliding the work face down on the fence and drilling successive holes every ¼ in. or so until I reach the other end. Toward the bottom of each hole, I slow down and use light pressure on the drill-press arm.

CUTTING THROUGH THE MORTISES AND MAKING THE TENONS

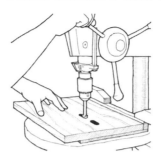

STEP 1

Back up workpiece with clean scrap; use a Forstner bit to remove most of the waste. Set depth stop so bit just cuts through stock.

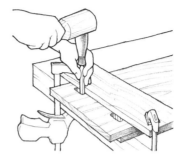

STEP 2

Guide chisel with a straight piece of scrap, and pare remaining waste from walls of the mortise.

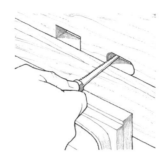

STEP 3

A shopmade saw used like a rough file squares the corners. Carefully work the saw into the corner.

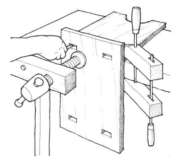

STEP 4

Transfer mortise location to tenon stock. Use a knife or sharp pencil to mark out the tenon width.

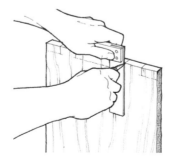

STEP 5

Extend tenon layout lines down the face of the stock with a square.

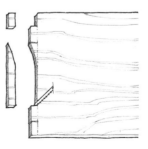

STEP 6

Mark the length of the tenons with a marking gauge or knife, and then cut to the line on a bandsaw.

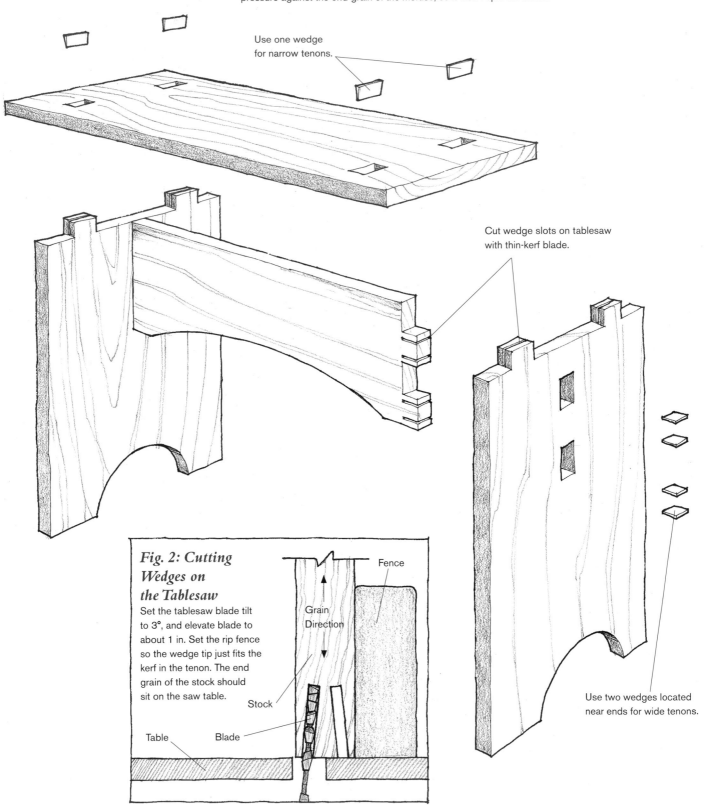

Fig. 1: Wedge Direction

Wedges spread the tenon and lock the joints together. The wedge should exert pressure against the end grain of the mortise, so it won't split the stock.

Use one wedge for narrow tenons.

Cut wedge slots on tablesaw with thin-kerf blade.

Use two wedges located near ends for wide tenons.

Fig. 2: Cutting Wedges on the Tablesaw

Set the tablesaw blade tilt to 3°, and elevate blade to about 1 in. Set the rip fence so the wedge tip just fits the kerf in the tenon. The end grain of the stock should sit on the saw table.

Fence

Grain Direction

Stock

Table   Blade

Shopmade Saw Cleans Out Corners

After roughing out the mortise on the drill press, I trim up those little waves on the sides and any remaining waste on the bottom of the mortise with a sharp chisel. This can be done by eye, but you'll get better results if you clamp a straight piece of ¾-in.-thick scrap across the workpiece to serve as a guide (see step 2 on p. 51). You can use the guide to square up the corners by working toward the corner from one direction and then swinging the guide 90 degrees and working in from the other. If you use a chisel to square up the corners, be sure to work in from both sides of the workpiece, or you'll tear out some really nasty chipping on the back side.

The way I square up the corners is to saw them out with a small, stiff saw (see step 3 on p. 51). I made my saw by filing teeth into the back of a carbon-steel paring knife. But you could also modify a wallboard saw by hammering the teeth flat, filing the sides of the blade to remove all set and then filing the teeth straight across like a rip saw.

I lay the saw against the wooden guide clamped to the workpiece and saw to the corner of the mortise. I use the saw as a rough file to square out the corners (there will be minor tearout on the back side).

Lay Out and Cut the tenons

I mark the tenon directly from the mortise using a small knife or pencil sharpened to a chisel point. Because the tenon thickness is the full-stock thickness, only the width must be marked (see step 4 on p. 51). I use a square to extend this line down the face of the stock (see step 5 on p. 51) and a marking gauge to scribe the tenon length. The tenon should extend completely through the mortised stock with an extra ⅟32 in. or so. This will be trimmed flush later, after the wedges have been glued in place.

I bandsaw the tenons using the cutting sequence shown in step 6 on p. 51. If all goes well, the tenons will fit snugly into the mortises on the first try. This never happens for me, though, so some fitting is usually required. Filing either the mortise or the tenon usually will take care of a too-tight fit. If you have some gaps, don't worry. Small shims cut from the same stock will hide them.

Cutting Wedges and Assembly

After fitting the mortises and tenons, I cut the wedge slots in the tenons. A thin-kerf cutoff blade in a tablesaw will produce a clean slot that's about the right width. Depending on the size of the tenon and its direction in the mating stock, I use one or two wedges to spread the tenon and create a tight joint.

Wedges should always exert pressure against the end grain of the mortise to keep the workpiece from splitting. I locate the slots as shown in figure 1 on the facing page.

I saw the wedge material by ripping the stock, on edge, on the tablesaw, as shown in figure 2 on the facing page. I angle the blade at 3 degrees, and adjust the fence until the point of the wedge will just fit into the kerfs I've sawed into the tenons. I cut the wedge material to length, and now I'm ready to assemble the joint. After clamping everything together, I drive the wedges home with a bit of glue on the leading edge.

JIM RICHEY works wood in Katy, Texas, and is the "Methods of Work" editor for *Fine Woodworking* magazine.

Master the Miter

BY GARY ROGOWSKI

The attraction of a miter joint is easy to see. It is an elegant and straight-forward method for joining parts that meet at an angle without showing any end grain. Whether you are building the frame for a veneered panel (tabletops, case goods), applying wraparound molding or constructing a simple picture frame, a miter joint will serve your needs. But as the saying goes, the devil is in the details. The very visibility of the miter joint means that errors in machining or assembly are hard to conceal. However, with a little patience and lots of practice cutting and assembling miters, you too can master the joint.

Generally used for right-angle corners between two boards of equal thickness and width, miters are made with matching cuts. These cuts are at 45 degrees so no end grain shows. But the miter joint isn't reliable solely as a glue joint for most constructions. Where any real tenacity is required, strengthening with biscuits, splines, or keys is always the prudent choice. In short, to get perfect miters requires perfectly mating joints, a slip-proof gluing system, and at least one form of strengthening.

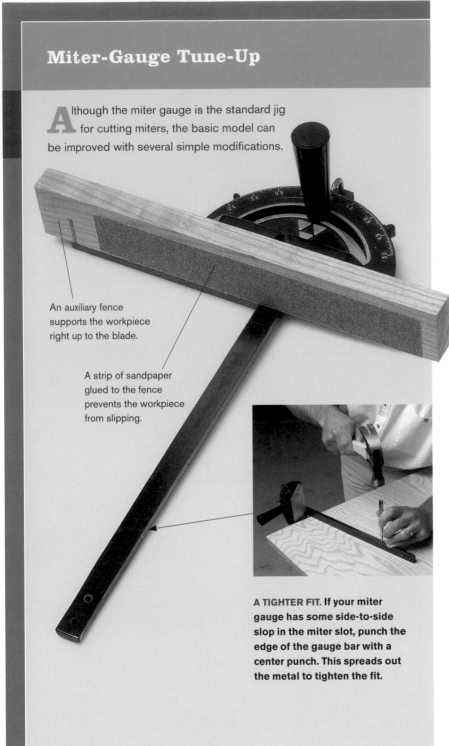

Miter-Gauge Tune-Up

Although the miter gauge is the standard jig for cutting miters, the basic model can be improved with several simple modifications.

An auxiliary fence supports the workpiece right up to the blade.

A strip of sandpaper glued to the fence prevents the workpiece from slipping.

A TIGHTER FIT. If your miter gauge has some side-to-side slop in the miter slot, punch the edge of the gauge bar with a center punch. This spreads out the metal to tighten the fit.

Cut Miter Joints with a Chopsaw or Tablesaw

No matter what type of saw you cut miters with, use a sharp, clean blade. Generally the more teeth to a blade, the smoother the cut, but no blade will cut well if it's dull or covered with pitch. Every cut is made in two directions: at 45 degrees across the width of a board and at 90 degrees across its face. For a miter to close up well, both angles need to be cut exactly. Make rough adjustments using a plastic 45 degree drafting triangle, then take several practice cuts, checking the results with a combination square.

A chopsaw works great at cutting miters. Just make sure the fence is flat and straight. If necessary, add an auxiliary fence and shim it to make it square to the table. Frame parts can lie flat on the chopsaw table. Angle the blade 45 degrees to the fence to make the cuts. Clamp stops onto the auxiliary fence to index matching cuts. When cutting miters on a tablesaw, you'll get the best results using a jig that holds your work to move it past the blade.

The miter gauge is, of course, the standard jig used for cutting miters. Be sure to check your settings for the angle of cut (see the photos on p. 54). Attach an auxiliary fence to the miter gauge to support the workpiece near the blade.

When cutting frame miters, angle the gauge down and away from the blade. This way, if the workpiece slips, it will slide away from the blade, not into it. A piece of sandpaper glued to the fence will help prevent slipping. Make certain that your gauge is cutting a true 45 degree angle, then cut one end of each matching part. Measure and mark off the required length and clamp a stop onto the auxiliary fence to index the cut so matching parts are the same length.

Make a Test Cut and Check for Square

TO SET THE MITER GAUGE AT EXACTLY 45°, first align a drafting triangle against the miter slot in the tablesaw (left). Make a cut in a piece of scrapwood (center). Flip over the cutoff piece and hold both pieces tightly against a square (right). Adjust the miter gauge until there is no gap, and you are set to cut perfect miters.

Picture-Frame Jig Ensures Accuracy

A picture-frame jig has four parts: a flat base, two runners, a fence, and clamping blocks. The base can be made of any flat ½-in.-thick sheet stock. Make the runners, which attach to the bottom of the base, out of quartersawn hardwood, so seasonal movement won't affect their fit.

The fence of the jig is ¾-in.-thick plywood. Cut the corner of the fence at a right angle, then screw it to the base. It won't matter if it's mounted a little off a true 45 degree angle as long as you always cut one piece of the miter joint on the left side of the fence and the other on the right side. The cuts will always be complementary and mate perfectly. Put on the clamping blocks last. You can clamp a stop block to these blocks to make cuts of uniform length.

Fine-Tune the Fit Before Glue-Up

After cutting the miters, do yourself a favor and take some time to prepare them for gluing. First check your cuts to see how well your saw performed. There are several ways to remedy a cut that is less than smooth. Trim the miter with a low-angle block plane, tuned up with a freshly sharpened blade. Put the workpiece in a vise and take a few light passes off each mating face, but don't change the angle. Check your results with a combination square.

A disc sander outfitted with a miter-gauge jig can also be used to fine-tune miters. This jig rides in the slot in the sander table and has a plate on it cut at 90 degrees but positioned 45 degrees to the sanding disc. Work on both sides of this fence to ensure that mating pieces get complementary cuts, but always work on the left side of the moving disc. In this way your work will always get pushed down into the supporting table.

Picture-Frame jig

Cut adjoining parts on opposite sides of the jig to guarantee a 90° joint.

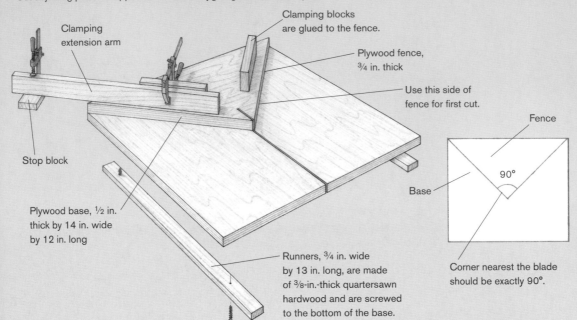

Clamping extension arm

Clamping blocks are glued to the fence.

Plywood fence, ¾ in. thick

Use this side of fence for first cut.

Stop block

Plywood base, ½ in. thick by 14 in. wide by 12 in. long

Runners, ¾ in. wide by 13 in. long, are made of ⅜-in.-thick quartersawn hardwood and are screwed to the bottom of the base.

Fence

90°

Base

Corner nearest the blade should be exactly 90°.

1. THE FIRST CUT IS MADE on the left-hand side of the jig. If the work slips, it will do so away from the blade.

2. UNIFORM LENGTH. Mark the length on the workpiece and on the right-hand fence. Clamp a stop block against the mitered end.

3. MAKE THE SECOND CUT on the right-hand side of the jig. With the stop block in place, you are assured of consistent cuts.

Trimming Miters by Hand and Machine

A LIGHT PLANE. A few passes with a well-tuned block plane clean up the surface and alter the angle, wwif necessary.

ACCURATE SHOOTING. This shooting board, when used with a square-sided plane, trims the wood at 45° across its width and at 90° to its face.

SAND TO FIT. Another way to fine-tune a miter joint is to use a jig that holds the workpiece at 45° to a sanding disc.

Take only light passes, and try to move the work past the disc so you don't burn the wood or load up the disc in one spot. Before starting, double-check that the sander's table is exactly 90 degrees to the disc.

A third method of trimming is to use a shooting board. A stop angled 45 degrees on both sides is screwed to the base. When used with a square-sided plane, this jig will trim the miter at 45 degrees across its width and at 90 degrees to its face.

Gluing and Clamping Miters

SIZING THE JOINT. The open grain on the face of a miter should be sealed with a thin layer of glue and allowed nearly to dry. The sealed end grain won't starve the joint when glue is applied to connect the miter.

A BETTER BAND CLAMP. Plastic corner blocks added to a band clamp reduce the risk of crushing the corners of the workpiece.

BAR-CLAMP TECHNIQUES. Shopmade clamping blocks distribute pressure across the joint and won't mar the workpiece.

Even Clamping Pressure Is Critical

Wood is made up like a bundle of straws. Crosscut or miter the end of a board, and you expose the ends of those straws, which suck up glue and starve a joint, weakening it. The faces of a miter joint should be sized by precoating them with a light wash of glue to fill the pores. Scrape off any excess glue before it dries. Despite the normal warning not to apply glue to an already glued surface, in this case sizing will strengthen the glue joint.

Dry-fit and clamp everything before the final glue-up, and you'll thank yourself later for your calm demeanor and slow heart rate. Mind you, I am a yellow-glue devotee, so all of this advice comes from using quick-setting glue, not some expansive, messy polymer.

Band clamps fit around a box or a picture frame to apply even pressure to the miter joints. Practice locating and tightening the band clamp in place right over the joint. Use several clamps for wider glue-ups, and stagger the clamp heads so they're not in each other's way.

You can put clamping corners over the joint to help spread the pressure. Some band clamps come with self-adjusting corners suitable for any angle; you can also buy aftermarket versions. Again, practice with these systems before gluing.

When gluing up miters with splines or keys that would interfere with a band clamp, I use shopmade clamping blocks clamped right onto the frame side. These blocks have a notch cut right into them where you can place another clamp to apply pressure directly across the joint. If your clamping blocks slip too much, glue a piece of sandpaper to them on the side that rests against the workpiece.

How to Strengthen Miters

Reinforce miter joints by using splines or biscuits, which are inserted before the joint is glued up, or keys, which are added after glue-up. Which method you use is determined by several factors, the most important being aesthetic considerations. Do you want to conceal the strengthening for a seamless look, as with a gilded picture frame, or do you prefer to emphasize it, as with face-frame keys? The second factor is the difficulty and length of time involved.

Splined miters in frames Through spline cuts are made along the length of the miter. They're most easily made on the tablesaw. Use a spline-cutting jig to support the workpiece at a 45 degree angle to the blade. Make this jig out of a straight piece of ¾-in.-thick plywood and a support piece glued and screwed on at a 45 degree angle. Make certain that your fasteners are higher than the tablesaw blade at its highest setting.

With your frame piece in the jig, set the fence so that the sawkerf is centered in the thickness of the stock. If it's not, the faces of your frame members will not be flush. One way to prevent this is by having a miter jig with two fences on it for each side of the miter (see the photos and drawings on pp. 62–63). The jig is rotated 90 degrees to cut the spline in the adjoining workpiece.

Set the blade height for a ¼-in.- to ⅜-in.-deep cut, but no deeper. Because the grain direction of a spline in a solid-wood frame has to run in the same direction as the frame members, too deep a spline cut makes for a wide and fragile spline. Hold or clamp the work firmly in the jig. Place your hands carefully out of harm's way and make a pass. Use a flat-grind blade to put a flat bottom on the cut.

Mill up the spline material out of a contrasting wood to set off the joint. Using a tenoning jig, hold the board vertically and run it past the blade to trim your spline to thickness. Then cut the spline to length. If your spline doesn't quite fit, use a block plane to trim it to thickness. Be careful not to snap the short grain of the spline as you plane. You're looking for a snug fit, not one that's overly tight.

Fit one side of the spline and check to see that it will let the joint close up nicely. Trim its end grain with a block plane, if needed. Size the end grain of the miter, then put glue in one of the spline cuts with a thin piece of wood. Set the spline in place all the way down to the bottom of the groove. Then put glue on the rest of the joint and clamp it up. If the fit is a bit loose, clamp across the face of the joint as well. You can also pin this spline in place with dowels for extra strength and an additional design detail.

Biscuit splines You can also strengthen a miter with a biscuit joint. Mark the frame members across their faces with a pencil at the center of the joint or closer toward the inside corner of the joint so that the cut won't show at the corners. Center the joiner in the thickness of the stock. Support or clamp the frame members securely, and hold the joiner tight to the miter as you cut.

Keys Can Reinforce Miter Joints

Mitered frames may also be reinforced after glue-up using exposed keys. These keys are inserted into mitered corners from the outside after cutting the appropriately sized slots. Slots may be cut on a tablesaw or on a router table.

Cutting straight keys on the tablesaw
Keyed miter jig works great for holding a glued-up frame in place while you pass it through the sawblade (see the photos and drawings on p. 64). Set the blade height for the full depth of cut, and use a flat-grind blade if you have one. Cut

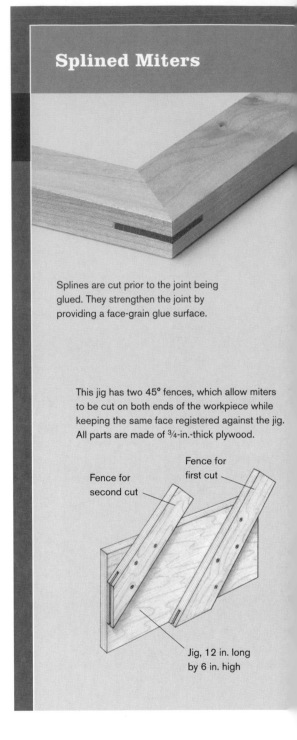

Splined Miters

Splines are cut prior to the joint being glued. They strengthen the joint by providing a face-grain glue surface.

This jig has two 45° fences, which allow miters to be cut on both ends of the workpiece while keeping the same face registered against the jig. All parts are made of ¾-in.-thick plywood.

Fence for second cut

Fence for first cut

Jig, 12 in. long by 6 in. high

each corner, holding the same face of the frame to the jig.

Mill up key stock wider than the depth of the key cut. Trim the stock to thickness on the tablesaw. You should use a thin push stick to help you move the work safely past the blade. Use a handplane to trim the key exactly to thickness, then cut it longer than necessary.

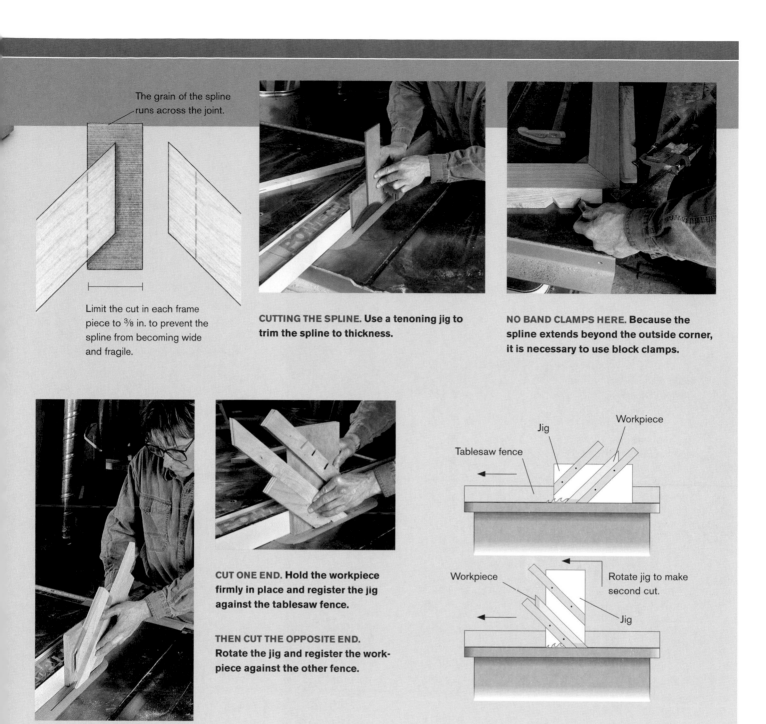

The grain of the spline runs across the joint.

Limit the cut in each frame piece to ⅜ in. to prevent the spline from becoming wide and fragile.

CUTTING THE SPLINE. Use a tenoning jig to trim the spline to thickness.

NO BAND CLAMPS HERE. Because the spline extends beyond the outside corner, it is necessary to use block clamps.

CUT ONE END. Hold the workpiece firmly in place and register the jig against the tablesaw fence.

THEN CUT THE OPPOSITE END. Rotate the jig and register the workpiece against the other fence.

Tablesaw fence

Jig

Workpiece

Workpiece

Rotate jig to make second cut.

Jig

Fit keys in their cuts so that they're snug and only require a light tap to position them. Make sure when gluing that they fit all the way down in the key cut at both its sides. Once the keys are dry, clean them up on the bandsaw. Sight along the edge of your frame as you make the cut so you don't cut into the piece. Then handplane away from the corner in each direction to trim the key flush. If you plane toward the corner, you will tear out the tip of the key.

Cutting face-keyed miters Face-keyed miters for frames probably originated when someone made a straight key cut in the wrong spot. It was a pretty mistake. Make these cuts using the keyed miter jig on the

Keyed Miters

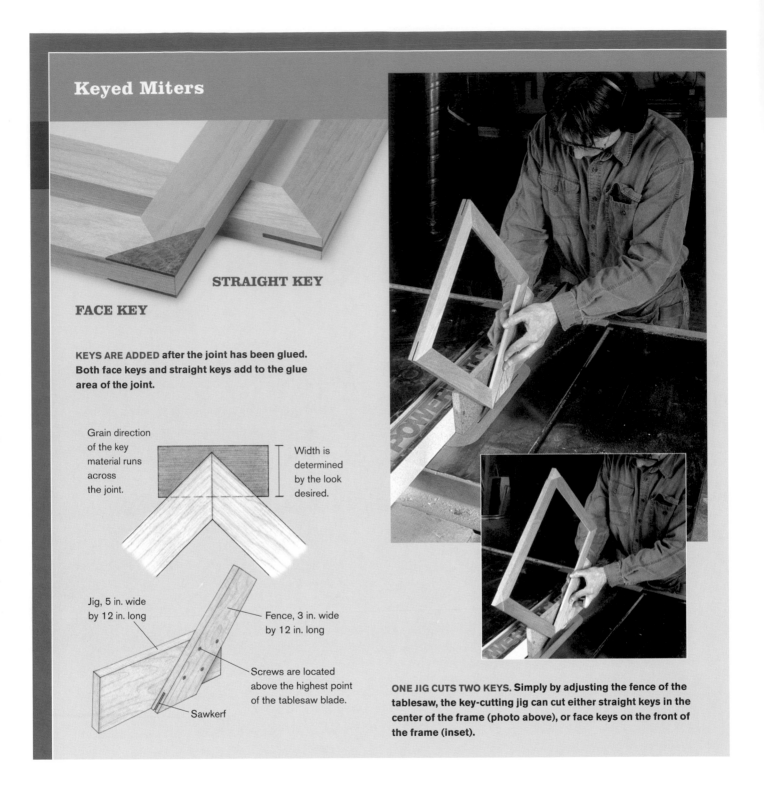

STRAIGHT KEY

FACE KEY

KEYS ARE ADDED after the joint has been glued. Both face keys and straight keys add to the glue area of the joint.

Grain direction of the key material runs across the joint.

Width is determined by the look desired.

Jig, 5 in. wide by 12 in. long

Fence, 3 in. wide by 12 in. long

Screws are located above the highest point of the tablesaw blade.

Sawkerf

ONE JIG CUTS TWO KEYS. Simply by adjusting the fence of the tablesaw, the key-cutting jig can cut either straight keys in the center of the frame (photo above), or face keys on the front of the frame (inset).

tablesaw. Place the cut just on the outside edge of each corner on both faces of the frame. Make up key stock as before, but this time just make it conveniently thick. When gluing, make sure the keys fit down to the bottom of the cut on both sides of the joint. Put clamps across the keys to hold them in place. The final step is to plane the keys flush with the face of the frame, being careful of the contrasting grain directions.

GARY ROGOWSKI is a contributing editor to *Fine Woodworking* magazine and the author of *The Complete Illustrated Guide to Joinery*.

The Slip Joint

BY FRANK KLAUSZ

Some years ago, I went to see a show at the Metropolitan Museum in New York that featured artifacts from the tomb of the Egyptian king Tutankhamen. On display was a chair built around 1350 B.C., on which I could see a slip joint. There are reasons this joint has been in use for so long. Also called an open mortise and tenon, the slip joint is hard to beat for ease of assembly. And because of the large gluing area where the pieces meet, a slip joint holds up to a lot of stress.

I build and repair furniture for a living, so I'm interested in not only doing a job well but also doing it efficiently. Unless an architect or designer has supplied me with very detailed drawings, it is often up to me to decide what joinery to use for a given job. The slip joint is one of my favorites.

A JIG FOR MAKING SLIP JOINTS

This jig makes both mortises and tenons. A channel, sized to your tablesaw fence, keeps the jig running smoothly and safely.

Mount clamp with hanger bolt and wing nut.

Hanger bolt, washer, and wing nut

24 in.

24 in.

Brace, ¾ in. by 1½ in.

Channel for tablesaw fence

Staggered holes in the back piece allow the clamp to be moved for different-sized stock. The back piece will be cut repeatedly by the sawblade, so build the jig so that the piece can be replaced.

QUICK CLAMP

The eccentric clamp holds any thickness of stock tightly. The offset hole makes the clamp act as a cam.

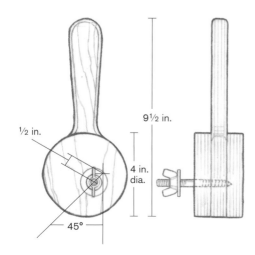

½ in.

9½ in.

4 in. dia.

45°

Mortise

Cut the mortise first. With the clamp, secure the piece of stock to be cut firmly into the back corner of the jig. Make the first cut. Remove the stock, flip it around, reclamp it and make the next cut. Depending on the size of your slip joint, two passes are usually enough to complete the mortise. The one shown at left took three passes at two fence settings.

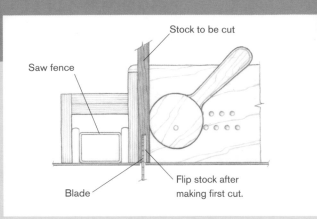

Stock to be cut

Saw fence

Blade

Flip stock after making first cut.

A doweled butt joint may go together faster, but it's not nearly as strong.

Where to use it? If I have a cabinet that calls for simple frame-and-panel doors, where rails and stiles are square-edged and the doors are inset, I don't have to think twice about which joint to use. For overlay doors, where the edges will show, I'd still use a slip joint, although I'd ask the clients

first whether they had any objections to seeing end grain on the outside of the stile.

When I make a chair, I use this joint for the slip seat that gets upholstered and secured within the chair rails (see the photo on p. 65), because it's the best and most appropriate joint for the job. I don't do a lot of millwork, but if I were making a window sash, I'd use a slip joint for the stiles and

Tenon

Change the setting from mortise to tenon. Use the mortised piece to reset the fence for the tenon cuts. Set the blade to cut on the other side of the cheek line. Always use scraps to test this fit. Once the fence is set, cut one side of the tenon, flip the piece in the jig and cut the other. Cut off the waste at the shoulder line later, using a miter gauge and a stop block.

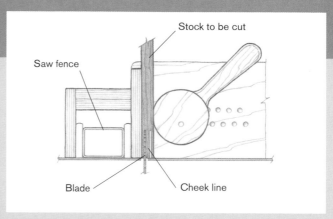

Stock to be cut

Saw fence

Blade

Cheek line

rails, even if the inside edges were shaped to a cope-and-stick profile.

What I really like about the slip joint is how fast it is to cut and assemble. I use a jig that I designed several years ago for use on my tablesaw (see the drawing on p. 65). If you don't have a tablesaw, you can cut this joint by hand or with a bandsaw, as I'll explain later. With either of these methods, take your time. If you use a bandsaw, make sure that the blade doesn't wander.

Cutting Mortises on the Tablesaw

Whether you build a jig similar to mine or use a system of your own, start with the mortise when cutting this joint on the tablesaw. The beauty of this system is that you don't have to spend any time marking all the pieces with a gauge or pencil. The setup for the mortise is done by eye, and the tenon cuts are taken directly from the mortise.

When I was an apprentice, I learned to determine the thickness ratios of the mortise and tenon by dividing the stock into thirds. So a board ¾ in. thick would have a tenon ¼ in. thick, give or take. You can estimate the mortise dimensions without having to measure them. All that matters is that the pieces fit together well when you're done. I always make sure to keep some scrap pieces of wood on hand for setting up and testing the joints before I use the stock I've milled for the job. Test pieces should be of the same thickness and width as the stock you'll use later.

CHEEK CUTS FOR THE TENON
To test the tenon setup, cut the cheeks first. The height of the sawblade off the table does not change. One pass per side is sufficient.

SHOULDER CUTS FOR THE TEN-
ONS ARE **best done with a miter
gauge. A scrap clamped to the
fence acts as a stop. Self-stick
aluminum carbide sandpaper
on the miter gauge keeps stock
from slipping.**

I make the first setup by cranking the sawblade up to the width of the stile. I place the jig over the top of the saw fence, which serves as a guide track, and clamp in a piece of scrap. I adjust the saw fence so that it's cutting into the middle third of the thickness of the wood. Then I push the piece through, flip it in the jig and push it through again. The first mortise is done. With the mahogany frame shown in the photos, my first setup left me with a sliver of waste between the first and second passes. I decided to leave it like that—making the tenon a little fat of one-third—and to make a second fence adjustment later to clean out the mortise (see the photo on

p. 67). Once I'm satisfied with the setup on the test piece, I can go ahead and cut all the mortises.

One important point: Keep your saw table free of debris that would prevent the wood from riding flat on the table. Also, be sure to clamp the wood firmly in the back of the jig. Losing track of either of these details will cause the mortises to be cut too shallow and out of square.

Cutting the Tenons

After cutting all the mortises, I turn off the saw, leaving the last mortised piece clamped in the jig. I loosen the fence and tap it lightly toward the blade by the amount of

Making the Slip Joint by Hand

MARK THE SHOULDER LINE. All pieces cut by hand must be marked on every side and end.

MARK MORTISES AND TENONS AT THE SAME SETTING. Fill in the scribed lines with pencil marks, so the lines are easier to read.

Cutting mortises and tenons by hand is neither as fast nor as accurate as the tablesaw method. But if you don't have the equipment or just prefer the look of handwork, this may be the way for you.

I start by looking over my milled pieces, deciding which will be the show faces and indicating that with a pencil mark. I save some marking time by ganging pieces together when I lay out the joints (see the near photo at right). I pencil in the shoulder line on the edges of four pieces at the same time and transfer those lines all the way around all the pieces. I then set my marking gauge to scribe the cheek lines (see the second photo at right). Mortises and tenons are marked with the same gauge setting. I just cut on different sides of the line—inside for mortises, outside for tenons. When I'm shaping this joint by hand, I always start by doing all the sawcuts first.

For the long cuts starting on the end grain, I prefer to use a wide-blade bowsaw (one of several my father made for me years ago when he came from Hungary to visit me). I clamp pieces in the vise in pairs to stiffen them and to make the process go a little faster. Remember to cut along the waste side of the marking-gauge line. I start the bowsaw at about a 45° angle to have a better view of what I'm doing. I cut straight down the marked lines to the shoulder lines drawn in pencil (see the left photo on the facing page).

To finish cutting the tenons at the shoulder line, I use a fine dovetail saw while holding the pieces against a bench stop, as shown in the photo at right. I am very careful to cut precisely to the waste side of each shoulder line. This is

important. Otherwise, I may end up with uneven tenon shoulders and a joint that will have to be adjusted later.

After the sawcuts have been made, mortises must be chiseled from both sides. I keep the flat of the chisel true to the marked pencil line as I remove the material. I cut halfway through the first side and then flip the piece over and work in from the other edge. A good size chunk will often pop out in one piece when working the second side. When all the mortises are done, I begin fitting the pieces together. This process takes a while.

Handwork is handwork—it's just not as precise as machined joinery and you're bound to have some adjustments to make. You may have to remove some material from a too-fat tenon or from the inside of one of the mortise cheeks, depending on how the joint fits together. Rasps and paring chisels will perform well for those tasks (see the bottom right

the blade thickness (⅛ in. for most saws), as shown in the photo on p. 67. With this setup, the cheek line of the mortise is cut on the inside of the sawblade, closest to the fence; the cheek line of the tenon is cut on the outside of the blade. Once the jig is at the new setting, I remove the workpiece and clamp in a fresh piece of scrap for a test tenon. I run the piece through the saw, turn it around and run it through again.

At this stage, I usually chop off the waste around the tenon, without marking it, to see if the tenon fits snugly into the mortise. (A handsaw or bandsaw works well.) I once asked my grandfather how tight this joint should be. He said, "If you need a mallet to force it, it is too tight and will split, but if you can use your hat instead of a mallet, it is too loose."

After these cuts have been made, the waste on either side of the tenon must

THE BOWSAW is Klausz's tool of choice for cutting this joint by hand because the long, wide blade tracks well and cuts quickly.

CUT THE SHOULDERS WITH A DOVETAIL SAW. For well-fitting joints, make sure that you cut to the same line on all the pieces.

FINE-TUNE THE FIT. Rasps and chisels are good choices for removing material from either the tenon or the mortise. Hand-cut frames need many test runs before you can call them done.

photo above). If you cut the tenons too thin and the mortises too wide, you can add shims of veneer (preferably of the same species) as gap fillers when you reach the glue-up stage.

Assembly and glue-up: I use a white PVA glue, applying it with a ½-in. acid brush. After I've dry-fit and adjusted the frame, I apply the glue evenly on all sides of all pieces. Then I put clamps loosely on each corner, using the scraps from cutting the tenons to protect the frame pieces. After that, I check the frame for squareness and make sure all the shoulders are

tight. Then I tighten the clamps all the way, make a final check for squareness, wipe off any excess glue with a wet rag and put the frame aside to dry. Later, I'll clean up the edges with a plane, working in from the corners to avoid chipout.

I remember once as a young man watching my father work, asking him, "How can you do that so fast?" He replied, "Don't worry. After five or 10 years, you're going to be a good beginner yourself." And now, after 46 years, I'm still learning.

be removed. I do that with the stock flat on the table. I remove the jig and dial the sawblade down to the right height to trim off the waste. I always clamp a stop block against the fence to serve as an index for trimming the cheeks to the exact shoulder line. The stop block also prevents the waste from being pinched between the fence and the blade. The miter gauge works well for this operation. Getting this setup tuned

correctly may take a few tries with scrap pieces, but the final trimming goes quickly. One tip—save your cutoff scraps as protective pads for gluing up the frames.

FRANK KLAUSZ is a cabinetmaker who makes and restores furniture in Pluckemin, New Jersey.

In Search of the Right Mortising Technique

BY STROTHER PURDY

MAN OR MACHINE. Everyone can find a way to cut mortises well, whether through improving skills or finding a better tool. Some prefer the quiet approach of the chisel (above), and others go for the fast and furious router (right). Other good options include the drill-press-and-chisel approach, hollow-chisel-mortise machines and dedicated slot mortisers.

The first mortise I cut looked as though a miniature dynamite charge had been set off inside the board. Splinters pointed out of the hole in every direction. Inside, my chisel had mashed out nooks, crannies, and side passages instead of cutting the straight, flat and square hole I intended. It was plain to see that I had not been born with the skills to chop mortises by hand.

For a while I contemplated buying my way out of learning this skill. Though a good craftsman never blames his tools, I reasoned, a smart one tries to use the best one for the job. My tool wish list, however, was long and underfunded. A jointer and a planer had higher priority than a plunge router or a hollow-chisel mortiser.

In time I learned to cut mortises by hand with reasonable speed and pretty good results. It took a while, but I found I enjoyed the work. The mortises didn't look too hot, but the assembled joint eventually hid them from discerning eyes. I did wonder how strong they were. I knew that yellow glue did not hold across or fill gaps. This told me the uneven fit of my mortise-and-tenon joints couldn't be very strong. Sure, they held together when I tried to pull them apart, but I had no way to test them for the years of use and abuse I wanted them to withstand. It was time to find out how well the mortise had to fit the tenon to stay together and then learn how to cut them that way.

Good Design, Fit and Glue Make Strong Mortises

I asked Carl Swensson, a woodworker with more than common knowledge about joinery, what made a mortise-and-tenon joint strong. His lengthy reply, which lasted several days, was both enlightening and frustrating.

Boiled down, a strong joint is the product of balanced design (so that one member isn't stronger than the other), an accurate fit

What Makes a Good Mortise?

That's simple: a clean surface for a strong glue bond and a tight fit with the tenon.

THE FIT SHOULD BE

Not too tight: If you have to hammer the joint together, it's too tight. You'll likely split the mortise if you tap aggressively.

Not too loose: You shouldn't be able to move the tenon in the mortise at all or feel any back-and-forth movement when you try.

But just right: The tenon should fit into the dry mortise with hand pressure only. It should not come apart easily, and it certainly should be able to withstand gravity. A good fit may even need light mallet taps to drive the joint apart.

FOR A STRONG GLUE BOND, THE MORTISE CHEEKS SHOULD BE

- flat and smooth, so they meet the tenon evenly.
- unfinished, so the glue can penetrate the mortise cheeks.
- free of loose fibers, which would soak up the glue and not allow it to penetrate solid wood.

and a good glue bond. Everybody knows that glue will make a joint stronger. Swensson was the first who could tell me why. When a joint is under stress, the glue bond spreads it across the cheeks of the mortise and tenon. In a joint without glue, such as one that's only pegged or wedged, the stress will concentrate along edges and at points. This means that the fit must be tight in these places. In a glue joint, the fit is still important, but the accuracy and quality of the glue surfaces are crucial.

To find out more about glue bonds and their requirements, I spoke with Mike Witte, a technical manager at Franklin International. He sent me several manuals about glue, which I read in spite of the great risk of falling asleep. To bond at their full strength, almost all glues need a smooth-but-unburnished surface, free of loose fibers, because glue needs to penetrate a few thousandths of an inch into intact wood. If the surface is burnished—by a dull router bit, for example—the glue can't seep into the pores and has little grip. If the surface is covered with loose fibers, such as a dull chisel might leave, the glue attaches to the loose fibers and not the joint walls. The lesson here is that sharp tools increase joint strength.

Witte confirmed a sobering rule about glue joints: For the glue to do its job, the gap between mortise and tenon should not exceed 0.005 in. This sounded like something I'd need a computer numerically controlled (CNC) router to achieve. However, the way to get these kinds of tolerances really isn't by measuring but by feel. If a mortise and a tenon go together easily, don't need to be hammered home, yet don't come apart without effort, Witte claims they'll be within 0.005 in. apart (see the sidebar on p. 73).

Use Chisels for Low-Cost But High-Skill Mortising

Chisels are the ubiquitous mortising tool. Everybody has them, but many woodworkers don't use them because they require superlative skill to handle, and they are slow. I found that the first complaint is a half-truth, and the last is, well, true.

I visited Brian Boggs at his chair shop in Kentucky to see whether the humble mortising chisel and mallet were capable of cutting with the precision that glue manufacturers required. When he greeted me, the fact he held a mortising chisel in one hand and a micrometer in the other answered my question. Boggs's recipe is simple: The quality of the mortise depends largely on how the chisel is tuned. Boggs told of the occasion when a student who could not chop a good mortise borrowed his chisel and had no further problems.

MORTISING CHISEL AND MALLET.
Brian Boggs chops a mortise in a chair leg. Though it's the slowest way to cut a mortise, he derives great pleasure from chopping precise joints with good tools.

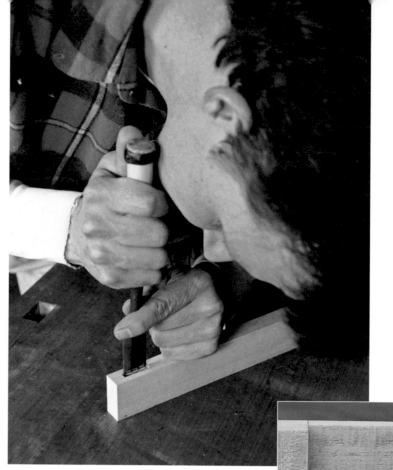

DRILL AND PARING CHISEL. Carl Swensson uses a drill press to quickly hog out the mortise waste (above), then a paring chisel to shave off the ridges left by the twist drill. Easy to see, the ridges make excellent guides for paring the mortise cheeks square and flat.

Mortising chisels generally have long, stout blades as thick or thicker than they are wide. This allows them to be hammered aggressively and deeply into hard woods without breaking. Unlike most power tools, few chisels arrive from the factory ready to go. To tune one, use an engineer's square to check the surfaces and a benchstone to make them true. The bottom and sides of the blade must be flat and square (the top of the blade is irrelevant). The cutting edge must be razor sharp, straight, and perpendicular to the sides. If not, the chisel will wander no matter how hard you try to keep it going straight down. Never hone a mortising chisel's edge on a buffing wheel because it will round the corners of the blade, right where it should be sharpest to cut the mortise walls.

Boggs begins a mortise by scoring his layout lines with bench chisels to keep splinters from running. He then removes an even ¹⁄₁₆ in. depth across the whole mortise. This creates a shoulder for the chisel to register against. The amazing thing is that

a well-tuned mortising chisel is almost self-guiding after the first ¹⁄₁₆ in.

Chopping down as far as the chisel will go in ⅛-in. increments, Boggs travels from one end of the mortise to the other and back again. The chisel's strong bevel breaks out chips as it cuts. Finally, he pares the cheeks lightly with a wide bench chisel.

Carl Swensson also cuts his mortises with chisels, but he begins on the drill press and finishes by paring the cheeks and ends with bench chisels. This method is slightly faster than chopping entirely by hand, but the drill press does take time to set up. Swensson drills a number of non-intersecting holes with a twist drill ¹⁄₃₂ in. thinner than the mortise is wide. The remaining waste between the drill holes is easily tapped out. The ridges left by the drill help him guide the chisel when paring the mortise walls flat and square (see the photos above).

It's rewarding work, but cutting mortises by hand is slow and tedious. Chisels do

have one important advantage over all other mortising tools, though, and that's their versatility. You can chop or pare a mortise of any size and shape anywhere on any piece of wood, which isn't always true of power tools.

Plunge Routers Cut Fast, Simple, and Precise Mortises

The router is to the woodshop what the microwave is to the kitchen. The two are fast, efficient, and versatile tools, but I always have a lurking suspicion they're bad for my health. The plunge router, however, is considered by many woodworkers to be one of the most useful tools for mortising.

Jeff Miller, a Chicago furniture maker and instructor, claims to have spent years sorting out the plunge router for mortising. It plunges accurately enough but doesn't move from side to side without help. It's also a top-heavy tool and needs a stable platform to ride on. The key to mortising small parts accurately with a plunge router, Miller found, was a simple, stable, and versatile jig to guide it—just a large block with clamps attached (see the photo above). The clamps hold the workpiece parallel to and even with the top of the block. The router rides on the block, and its fence registers on the opposite edge of the block.

For work that doesn't fit in the jig, the plunge router makes the journey to the workpiece with ease. John McAlevey, a Maine woodworker, uses a plunge router with a fence or a template to cut mortises that would be difficult with any other tool except a chisel and mallet.

Routers are capable of very smooth cuts, but not without some technique. They're light-duty tools, and even the monstrous 3-hp plunge routers need to be handled carefully and used gently. The jig or platform must be rigid to keep the router from wobbling. A bit plunged too fast or without wood on all sides will cut gouges down the mortise cheeks. Probably the best technique is to remove the waste in horizontal increments of $\frac{1}{32}$ in., moving the router slowly from end to end. An unstable jig or moving too fast will cause the bit to wander and cut steps in the mortise cheeks. An alternative is to plunge all the way down at either end of the mortise first. Then remove the waste in the middle. Both techniques will cut very clean mortises.

The price for the plunge router's speed is noise and dust I frankly don't enjoy using routers. They screech loudly and produce volumes of fine dust. Safety goggles, hearing protectors, and a good-quality dust mask help, but I dislike working in sensory deprivation gear, unable to hear the phone ring or see my work through the dust and scratches on my goggles. Nonetheless, I have to admit the speed of the router trumps its disadvantages. I watched McAlevey cut 14 mortises with a router in the time Carl Swensson cut three by hand.

Drilling Square Holes: Hollow-Chisel Mortisers

A dedicated hollow-chisel mortiser is a peculiar and wonderful tool, thereby typically English. In a nutshell, it's a specialized drill press with a hollow and square

PLUNGE ROUTER AND JIG.
The block-and-clamp jig gives the plunge router a stable base to cut quick and accurate mortises in small pieces.

Router Milling Jigs

A huge number of commercial jigs are available for the router, ranging from the simplest subbase to elaborate computer numerically controlled (CNC) rigs for the most ambitious hobbyist. Among them are a few interesting machines designed to turn the router into an all-purpose production milling tool. I'll call them router milling jigs for lack of a better term. They have names like Matchmaker, Mill-Right, and Multirouter. I've had the pleasure to see the Multirouter in action cutting mortises.

The Multirouter isn't hard to describe: It's a router jig gone mad (see the photo above). There are more levers, knobs, stops, setscrews, tables, and fences than any healthy woodworker should be asked to handle. But talking with Peter Turner, a Maine woodworker, made the jig seem devilishly easy to use.

The machine houses a standard fixed-base router in a frame that raises and lowers on linear bearings. The workpiece is clamped on a platform that moves from side to side and in and out. The platform also tilts, making angled work possible. It can cut mortises, tenons, dovetails, box joints, and anything in-between.

The great advantage of the machine is its speed in cutting more than a few mortises. The initial setup takes a while, but the adjustment for each operation is minimal. Once running, it can cut mortises in 15 seconds and tenons in less than 10. If you blink, you miss the process. Piles of parts for large casework can be milled in minutes. And the quality of the cut is excellent, though no better than any well-jigged router.

The main limitation is the price of the machine. Turner admits that he was not able to afford a new one, which costs about $2,300. But a bit of luck threw an inexpensive used one his way. He bought the machine with a friend, reducing his investment to a fraction of the cost of a new one.

chisel mounted around an auger bit. A quill feed plunges the spinning bit and hollow chisel into the workpiece, in effect drilling a hole and paring it square simultaneously. A series of these cuts produces a typical rectangular mortise.

Niall Barrett, a woodworker in upstate New York, owns a small one he's found to be a great mortising tool. It's reasonably quiet, fast, makes chips not dust and cuts square holes. With a price of about $300, it might seem the perfect mortising tool. However, these advantages come with a few problems. The drill-press-style setup limits the size of the workpiece to about 6 in. high. The workpiece must be rectangular in cross section, or it will be difficult to clamp firmly to the machine. The smaller-sized bits (¼ in. and ⅜ in.) heat up and burn or crack easily if misused. Finally, even when well-tuned, hollow chisels produce a moderately rough cut.

Barrett does not see the roughness as a problem, and he points out that he's never had a joint fail. I checked with another hollow chisel user, Tom Stangeland, a woodworker in Washington state, who agreed. It's a point well taken: After all, the perfect mortise is simply one that stays mated to its tenon. If the hollow-chisel mortiser cuts well enough, then it cuts perfectly well.

Industrial Advantages: Dedicated Slot Mortiser

Dedicated slot mortisers are industrial-grade machines with many advantages over the router and the commercial milling jigs. Slot mortisers have a horizontal drill-style head that slides forward and back, giving the cutter a plunging action. With all other methods, the piece stands still and the cutting tool moves. With slot mortisers, the workpiece is mounted on a sliding table that moves laterally to the head. This table can also be adjusted in height.

DEDICATED SLOT MORTISER
Chris Becksvoort cuts a slot for a mortise lock in a finished door. Unlike a router, a dedicated slot mortiser is quiet and a simple pleasure to use.

Slot mortisers cut very smooth, very accurate mortises even faster than a router (see the inset photo on the p. 76). They are surprisingly quiet—quieter than hollow-chisel mortisers—and produce chips not dust. They're made to withstand years of abuse without a whimper. And they're capable of almost any size or type of mortise in a workpiece that will fit on their bed. Maybe this is why I found, without looking very hard, several one-man shop owners who shelled out several thousand dollars to buy one. In the long term, the machines are simply worth it. Chris Becksvoort doesn't regret a penny he spent on his slot mortiser.

Besides using his slot mortiser for all the common mortises, Becksvoort uses his for end boring bedposts, lock holes in finished doors (see the photo above), and even cutting sliding dovetails in the bases of Shaker candle stands (a long story and a complex jig). Good technique is similar to routing a mortise, with one exception. To get the very best cut, Becksvoort raises the table a hair, recuts one face, then flips the workpiece and cuts the opposite face.

And the Right Tool Is . . .

With the dedicated slot mortiser, I found a compromise of speed, noise, and dust production that I really liked. The stumbling block, of course, is the price. Until I win the lottery, I'll putter along with my chisels, paying more attention to the sharpness of my tools and the fit of my joints. Chisels are hard to beat for their affordability and sheer pleasure of craftsmanship. Although this is my solution to making strong joints, I know much depends on personal preferences, so I don't necessarily recommend this route. I can make sacrifices of speed and ease to avoid noise and dust because I don't run a professional shop. If I did, I might get a plunge router or maybe a hollow-chisel mortiser. Unfortunately, each person I approached might have convinced me his tools and techniques were best, if I hadn't seen all the others.

STROTHER PURDY is a woodworker and former editor at The Taunton Press who lives in Bridgewater, Connecticut.

Tenoning Strategies

BY GARY ROGOWSKI

The mortise-and-tenon joint might be the most relied-upon joint in furniture making. After all, a well-fitted tenon can mean the difference between a sturdy table and an embarrassingly wobbly project. Cutting tenons can be approached from a dozen different directions, and the approach you take depends on your tools and how you like to use them. Some folks love the precision and power of their saw or router; others prefer the more contemplative whoosh of a backsaw and handplane. The method you choose will determine your speed and the risk factor.

A tenon should fit tightly in a mortise—snug, like a good shoe put on with a shoehorn—not like a ragged old sneaker that you can flip off and across the room as you're sitting down. Regardless of the cutting method you choose, aim for a joint that is loose enough to put together by hand but tight enough that it takes a few mallet taps to get it apart. Leave room for a little bit of glue in the joint, and always cut tenons just shy of the depth of the mortise so there's a gap at the bottom of the joint for excess glue.

Remember that accuracy comes from the patient hands of the builder and that precise joinery depends upon accurate millwork. If your millwork is sloppy—if your stock cups, warps or doesn't have parallel faces—you'll have trouble cutting accurate tenons, no matter what method you choose.

Also, I never cut mortises or tenons without first planning ahead on paper, even if it's just a quick sketch. It's better to risk a few simple eraser smudges on paper than to waste precious wood. A sketch will help you locate the joint for the most strength and best look. For strength, a tenon should be at least one-third the thickness of the stock to ensure there is enough material to support the joint.

Cutting Tenons by Hand

In these days of machines, it may seem a waste of time to cut a tenon by hand, but if you have only a few tenons to cut, you may be surprised by how much set-up time you can waste with some machines. When I have to cut only a few simple joints, I'll often reach for a backsaw and a shoulder plane.

Hand-cut tenons require careful setup and layout (see the photos on p. 84). Your method may involve using a marking gauge and square, a mortising gauge or a pencil and square. But whatever your method, be consistent with your approach and always be dead-on accurate. Even if you are using machines to cut tenons, the same guidelines for marking out hold true.

Use a marking gauge to mark the length of the tenon across its shoulders. Then establish the thickness of the joint by marking out the position and thickness of the tenon. If you cut a ½-in.-thick mortise in the center of a door stile, for example, lay out a ½-in.-thick tenon centered in the thickness of the door rail. Offset or unequal shoulders become necessary when two tenons meet inside a leg.

A marking gauge will lay out the cheeks of the tenon, but by running a mortise gauge along the face side of the joint, you can mark out both cheeks at once. Use the mortise to set the cutters on the gauge, then mark across the top and sides of the tenon. After cutting the tenon cheeks and shoulders, lay out the width of the tenon

and any haunch that is required (if you do this before cutting the cheeks and shoulders, the lines will be removed by the cheek cuts).

Use a backsaw to establish the shoulders. You want to cut right down to the cheek lines, but be careful not to saw past these marks.

Next, cut the faces of the cheeks. Placing the work in a vise allows you to see both the top gauge line and the cheek line nearest you. For a short tenon, cut straight down these lines until you reach the shoulder. For a longer tenon, angle the workpiece so that you can easily see the cheek lines. Cut down to the shoulder line on one side, then flip the piece around in the vise so that you can see the other cheek line as you cut down to it. Follow the cheek lines as you cut out the remaining wood in the middle of the tenon.

Cut one cheek of the tenon and clean it up with a bullnose or rabbet plane. Then move on to the second cheek and, if necessary, adjust its size before cutting. Or, if caution suits you, cut both cheeks a bit wide and then plane to fit. Once the thickness of

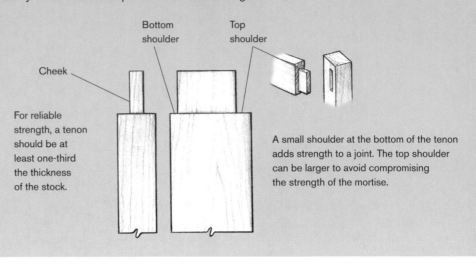

The Basic Tenon

If it takes more than hand pressure or a few light taps with a mallet, the fit of the tenon is too tight. And if there's too much slop, you're expecting too much of the glue you use. To ensure that the glue adheres well, make sure all faces are clean and smooth. Cut tenons just shy of the mortise depth to allow for excess glue.

Bottom shoulder

Top shoulder

Cheek

For reliable strength, a tenon should be at least one-third the thickness of the stock.

A small shoulder at the bottom of the tenon adds strength to a joint. The top shoulder can be larger to avoid compromising the strength of the mortise.

the tenon has been fine-tuned with a rabbet or bullnose plane, use the same methods to cut any haunches or other shoulders. Then grab a chisel and a plane to help you fit the tenon exactly to the mortise, trimming only a little at a time and test-fitting frequently.

Cutting tenons by hand doesn't take as long as you might think, and it is a great way to improve your hand-tool skills. Even as you turn to machines for efficiency, you'll find that it is often easiest to do the final fitting and cleanup with a chisel and plane.

Using the Radial-Arm Saw and Bandsaw to Cut Tenons

The radial-arm saw probably crosscuts more efficiently than any other machine, and the bandsaw rips better than any tool in my shop. You can take advantage of both features to save time cutting tenons (see Method 1 on p. 86). If you have a few

tenons to cut, use a pencil to mark out one tenon shoulder and cheek. Set a stop for the shoulder cut on the radial-arm saw table or fence. Adjust the depth of cut on the radial-arm saw and cut all of the shoulders to the proper depth.

Move to the bandsaw for the cheek cuts, and be sure to use a blade that suits your material. A 4-tpi (teeth per inch) blade works fine for most tenon cuts. But if you're cutting tenons in something hard like oak or mushy like green cedar, use a 3-tpi blade, which will push chips away and allow you to get through the cut more easily. On especially narrow tenons, a 6-tpi blade will work fine.

The bandsaw fence helps guide the cheek cuts. Set the fence so that the waste falls off harmlessly to the side instead of becoming trapped between the blade and fence. To play it safe you can clamp a stop onto the fence so that your cut ends before the blade runs into the shoulder. But

A TOUR OF TENONS

Whether you're building a chair or a desk or fitting together a frame-and-panel door, chances are there's a tenon designed to solve your joinery problems.

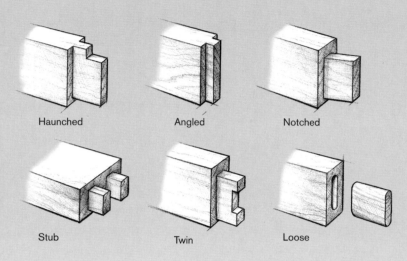

Haunched   Angled   Notched

Stub   Twin   Loose

with the shoulder cuts already established on the radial-arm saw, you should be able to stop when you push through the cut. If you don't have a fence, clamp a block of wood to the table at the proper distance to serve as a fence, or simply pencil-mark your cheeks and freehand the cut. Once you check for blade drift, angle your fence to match the drift angle. There still will be a little cleanup to do with a chisel and plane, but the bandsaw can get you pretty close.

Using this method, you can move the bandsaw fence over and cut the top and bottom of the tenon and any haunches. Then clean them up with a chisel.

Cutting Tenons Using a Tablesaw

By using various blade setups and jigs, there are several ways to cut tenons on the table-saw. When choosing a method, consider speed, safety and accuracy—and make sure the blades and jigs you use are running true.

A dado-blade setup for quick work

The fastest way to cut tenons using a tablesaw is with a dado blade (see Method 2 on p. 86). Set to the proper height, a dado blade will cut your cheeks and shoulders while you hold the stock flat on the saw table. Be careful while using a wide dado setup on the tablesaw, because these blades can take a big bite out of your board. Move slowly through the cut, and keep the board flat on the saw table.

Set up the blade for any reasonable width—it's really not that important. Crucial here are the height of the dado blade and how flat-bottomed a cut it makes. Take some practice cuts in scrap and set the blade height just under what you think you need. That way, there's just a little wood to remove for cleanup. Use a miter gauge with a long fence to push the board through the blade. You can mount an auxiliary fence on the miter gauge for better support, if needed.

Clamp a stop on the fence to locate the shoulder cuts.

Make the passes for one side of all of the boards first. If your blade cuts well, you'll need to clean these cheeks very little; but if your blade cuts like my dado blade, you'll have to take some time to plane the cheeks smooth. Then move to the second cheek cut and set the blade height for just under what you'll need.

After the tenon has been cut to its correct thickness, you can also use the same dado setup to cut a haunch or to establish the top and bottom shoulders of the tenon. Reset the blade height, rotate the stock in the miter gauge, and cut to fit. Approach these cuts carefully to make sure the shoulders line up.

Tenons cut vertically Because switching to a dado-blade setup takes some time, it doesn't always make sense for small jobs. The method I've used most often calls for a combination blade on the tablesaw (see Method 3 on p. 87). I cut the shoulders with a crosscut jig, rough-cut the cheeks on the bandsaw, then trim the tenons to fit perfectly by holding them vertically on the tablesaw and passing them through the blade using a shopmade tenoning jig.

Cutting the shoulders on a crosscut jig ensures accuracy from one tenon to the next. Set a stop on the jig fence closest to the shoulder. That way, if any dust gets stuck between the stop and the board, it pushes you away from the blade, not into it. (This problem can be remedied easily with another pass.) Next, rough out the tenons on the bandsaw. Everyone cuts a tenon undersized at some time or another. If you make this mistake, simply glue the perfectly matched offcut back on.

Make the cheek cut next with a shop-made tenoning jig. The jig I made is simply a piece of ½-in.-thick plywood with a stout right-angle fence screwed to it. The tenoning jig holds the workpiece vertically as I pass it through the blade. It probably took me five minutes to make the jig, and I've used the same one for years. Just make sure you keep the screws high enough in the fence that there's no risk of ever running them into the sawblade. Set the blade height so that it cuts just under the shoulder cut. Keep the board tight against the fence and jig either by hand or with a clamp, and make sure you don't tip the piece; otherwise, the tenon will have a taper cut into it.

Cut one cheek and check its placement by holding the cheek of the tenon against the face of the mortised piece. If the rail and stile are designed to be flush, you can see how close your first cut has come. If the mortise wall lines up with the face of the tenoned piece, you know your first cheek cut is perfectly placed. Then flip the board around and cut the cheek on the other side. If the tenon doesn't quite line up, you can also determine how much more you need to trim off the tenon cheek. If it covers the mortise wall so you can't see it all, you'll need to glue on one of those tenon offcuts from the bandsaw.

You can also use an aftermarket tenoning jig to make and fine-tune tenon cuts. It works the same way as my shopmade jig, but this metal jig has a screw-adjust system for very fine adjustments. It also locks the tenon stock in place for a safer cut. Just make sure there's no slop in the fit of this jig to your tablesaw slot.

You can cut haunches for tenons very simply with a single blade on the tablesaw. Clamp a stop on the crosscut-sled fence to locate the cut, and set the blade height for the proper depth of cut. Go back to the bandsaw to trim the haunch until it just fits inside the mouth of the mortise. On a smaller tenon, you can use the tenoning jig to make this pass.

For a Few Simple Joints, Cut Tenons by Hand

If you're cutting only a few small tenons, it can be faster (and quieter) to cut them by hand rather than to set up machines. No matter what method you use, careful layout is key.

MARKING OUT. A pass with a marking gauge (far left) lays out the depth of the tenon on all four sides; a mortise gauge marks the cheeks (left).

BACKSAW TO THE LINE. To cut both the shoulder and the cheek, first saw at an angle on each side (far left), then follow the kerf down the middle until the cut bottoms out (left).

TRIMMING FOR FIT. After a backsaw cuts the top and bottom shoulders of the tenon, a bullnose plane is used to clean up the cheeks (far left). A little handwork with a chisel trims the shoulder for a tight fit (left).

Three Ways to Cut Tenons Using Power Saws

With proper setup, almost any machine can cut tenons reliably. To achieve smooth joints and efficient working times, sometimes you have to use a combination of machines.

METHOD 1: CUTTING TENONS ON THE RADIAL-ARM SAW AND BANDSAW

RADIAL-ARM SAW establishes a shoulder kerf. The saw is set to the correct depth, and a stop block is clamped to the saw table. A single pass cuts a kerf on the tenon shoulder.

A BANDSAW TRIMS THE CHEEK. With the fence set in place, a quick pass cuts to the shoulder line. After adjusting the fence, another cut establishes the top and bottom of the tenon. A backsaw and chisel are used to clean up the shoulders.

METHOD 2: CUTTING TENONS ON THE TABLESAW

A DADO BLADE HOGS OFF THE WASTE. A stop block clamped to the fence sets the depth of the tenon while a miter gauge holds it square. Just a few passes over a dado blade cuts the tenon cheeks and shoulders. The same setup with the stock held vertically cuts the top and bottom of the tenon.

Cutting Tenons Using a Router Table

Given the proper amount of patience and set-up time, tenons can be cut successfully using a router table, and this setup really comes in handy if you have quite a few tenons to cut. This tenoning method is similar to the dado-blade setup on the tablesaw in that you need to set the bit height for a perfect cut. But with a good bit chucked in the router, you get a much smoother cut than you get with a dado blade on the tablesaw.

You can work the stock slowly toward the fence, or to save some wear and tear on your router bits, you can rough out the cheeks first on the bandsaw. Then set a

METHOD 3: CUTTING TENONS VERTICALLY

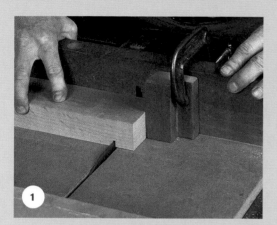

MAKING THE SHOULDER CUT. With a stop block clamped in place, a quick pass with a crosscut sled cuts the tenon shoulders (1). After a bandsaw hogs off the cheek waste, a tenoning jig–shopmade or aftermarket–holds the stock vertically to fine-tune the cut (2). Another pass with the crosscut jig cuts the top and bottom shoulder and any haunch (3).

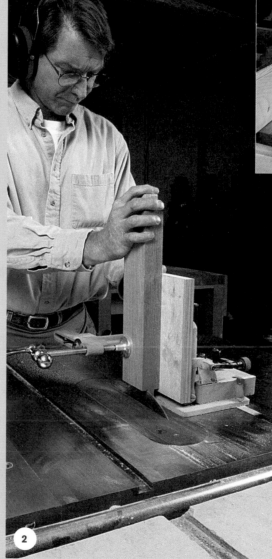

STORE-BOUGHT OR SHOPMADE. Aftermarket jigs, like the Delta at left, ride along the miter-gauge slot and secure the board vertically for tenoning, but the author often uses a simple shopmade jig (inset). The shopmade version is nothing more than a piece of plywood with a backer board screwed in place at a right angle.

fence for the proper shoulder distance, and set the bit height for the first cheek pass.

With a router table you can package two boards together for a more stable pass by the bit (see Method 1 on p. 88), or you can use a backer board to support the cut and to prevent tearout on the back of the cut where the bit emerges. Make the first cheek pass and then check it against the mortise. Raise the bit for a deeper cut. Even with a wide bit, it will take several passes to get back to the shoulder cut. This is an end-grain cut, which tends to burn when you cut too slowly, so move relatively quickly through the bit, making sure you don't leave uncut any patches of wood on the cheeks of the tenons.

Three Ways to Cut Tenons Using a Router

Whether you're cutting wide tenons or multiples of smaller tenons, a router leaves smooth faces that come off the machine ready for glue-up.

METHOD 1: ROUTER-TABLE TENONS

GANGING UP ON THE ROUTER TABLE. A router table allows you to gang up two or more boards, making fast work of cutting uniform tenons (left). If the mortises are cut with a router as well, the author uses chisels and files to round the tenon (center), checking his progress with a template routed to match the top and bottom of the mortise (right).

METHOD 2: PLUNGE-ROUTING WIDE TENONS

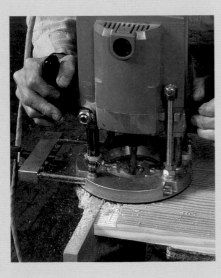  

AN EDGE GUIDE helps rout tenons on wide boards. When cutting breadboard ends or fitting a headboard to bedposts, wide tenons can be a beast to cut. A router with an edge guide (or registered against a temporary fence) does the job in a few passes (left). After the shoulder has been established, a backsaw and coping saw rough out notches to allow for wood movement (center), and a final pass with the router evens out the notch (right).

METHOD 3: PLUNGE-ROUTING LOOSE TENONS

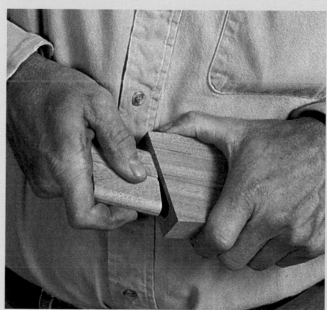

LOOSE TENONS FOR LONG STOCK. Sometimes lengthy boards are difficult to muscle around machines, but using loose tenons is a simple solution. A mortising template (left) guides a bearing-guided straight bit to cut mortises in both pieces you're trying to join. Tenon stock is cut to width and thickness, then the long edges are rounded (top photo) to fit the mortise. Short sections are trimmed to length and glued in place (above).

Tenoning Using a Router Machine

There aren't many faster ways to cut multiple tenons than with a horizontal routing machine. What's more, the same machine cuts mortises just as quickly. Though the prices can be high—these machines start at about $1,500—the time you save might be worth it.

STRAIGHT TENONS

ANGLED TENONS

ROUTING MACHINES for production work. Guided by templates or set by hand, the horizontal routing machine takes a little work to set up but can cut countless tenons in no time at all. The table also tilts to make easy work of angled tenons.

If you're cutting mortises using a router, you'll either have to square up the mortises or round over the tenons. When I opt to round over the tenons, I do it quickly with a chisel and file. A simple jig (nothing more than a short cut made with the router bit used for mortising) tells me when I've trimmed the tenon to the correct shape.

Plunge-Routing Tenons on Wide Stock

To cut tenons on a wide board, use a plunge router with a fence mounted on it (see Method 2 on p. 88). A breadboard end with multiple tenons is the perfect situation to use this method, but it also works well for narrow boards. You just have to package a few of them together to get better support for your router base.

Place a large-diameter straight or spiral bit in your plunge router and mount your fence to it. For better support, attach a longer auxiliary fence to the router fence. Fuss with the bit depth until you are pretty close to the final depth and then cut the first side of all of the cheeks. Work from the outside of the tenon in toward the shoulder, so you have good support for the router base. With thick stock, take several passes until you get to the correct depth and then move the router closer to the shoulder for the next series of passes. Save the shoulder cut as a final trim pass so you can concentrate on it being accurate. Move the router into the work from both edges to prevent tearout as you exit the cut.

Just like the other horizontal-cut methods, cut one cheek first and check to see that it's correct before moving to the second cheek. Because plunge routers typically have very fine adjustment features, it's pretty simple to take that second pass, check the fit and fine-tune as needed for a perfect fit.

Cutting multiple tenons on wide stock requires haunch cuts as well. Leave these cuts for last; this way, you can use the material to be cut away to test-fit against the tenons. Once the tenons fit, cut them to width on the bandsaw or with a handsaw. Reset the fence to cut the haunches to length, and set your bit for a full depth of cut. Plunge to depth and make the cuts, being sure you don't rout into the edges of the tenons. You'll be left with a round corner between the tenon and the haunch, which can be cleaned up with a chisel.

Plunge-Routing Loose Tenons on Long Stock

When your stock gets too long to cut tenons, you can use loose tenons (see Method 3 on p. 89), which are simply two mortises joined together with a long spline (for lack of a better word). The mortises are easy to cut using a mortising template and a plunge router mounted on a template guide. Make up loose-tenon stock out of the same material as your mortised pieces and trim it to fit in thickness (at the planer) and width (on the tablesaw). Then take it to the router table and, with a roundover bit, round the stock on all four long edges. Next, cut a glue-escape slot on the tablesaw before crosscutting it to length. When cut to length, the loose tenons should fit smoothly into the mortises.

Using a Horizontal Routing Machine to Cut Tenons

When a job calls for cutting a large number of tenons, it might be time to call out the big guns. When set up properly, a horizontal routing machine outfitted with a router can save you a lot of time and work. The machine does an excellent job of cutting a large number of tenons very quickly. You can use standard-sized tenon templates or design the joint to whatever dimensions you want. Another advantage is that the machine can cut angled tenons with ease simply by angling the worktable. But with prices starting at around $1,500, you have to be able to justify the cost of the machine.

Start by making a right-angle fence to locate all of the tenon pieces. With a simple, shopmade end stop, you can also set each tenon board in exactly the same location each and every time.

Mount a spiral-flute bit in the router and set its height to cut the tenon. Then set the table stops for both depth of cut and length of travel. With a good routing machine, cutting the tenon actually takes less time than the setup.

There are countless ways to cut tenons. The methods you choose should depend on the tools you have in your shop and on the number of tenons you have to cut. For a single small tenon, you can probably cut it quickly by hand. If you're cutting hundreds of tenons, a horizontal routing machine could save you hours and hours. For many of the jobs you encounter, you might find a happy medium with routers and saws. Just remember that what matters isn't how you cut tenons; it's how they fit.

GARY ROGOWSKI is a contributing editor to *Fine Woodworking* magazine and the author of *The Complete Illustrated Guide to Joinery*.

Double Mortise and Tenon Improves Strength

BY CRAIG VANDALL STEVENS

The mortise-and-tenon joint and its many variations have long been a preferred method for joining two pieces of wood at a right angle or close to it. One of my favorite versions is the double mortise and tenon. I use it to increase the strength of a joint on relatively small furniture parts, such as those on the freestanding room screen I built a few years ago. I knew the screen frame would be subject to some flexing in daily use, and I wanted to be certain that it would hold up to the stresses.

You'll often find the double mortise-and-tenon joint on chairs and window sashes—projects in which structural integrity on visually delicate pieces of wood is essential. By doubling the surface within a wood joint, you can greatly improve the joint's strength without increasing the size of its parts. What follows is an account of how I design and execute this joint. To cut the mortises I use a simple plywood jig and a plunge router equipped with an end-mill bit. For the tenons I use a combination of tablesaw, bandsaw, and chisels. Others may prefer another technique, such as doing the job entirely by hand or using a mortiser or drill-press setup. Any way you choose to cut it, the benefits of employing a double mortise and tenon in your work are worth the extra effort required.

Prepare the Stock with the End Use in Mind

I always start milling the lumber for a project several days ahead of time, then set it aside to stabilize. Initially, I flatten stock with a jointer and rip the individual pieces a bit oversized with the bandsaw. (I use a bandsaw rather than a tablesaw most of the time because it's a safer and quieter machine, and it produces less waste.) When the wood has stabilized, all of the pieces can be rejointed on two adjoining faces to flatten out any springback that has occurred and then brought down to their final thicknesses with a planer. It's always a good idea to mill some extra stock for setting up the joinery and to use as backups if you make a mistake along the way.

With furniture parts that will eventually be sized differently, I prefer to mill all of the stock to the same thickness, complete the joinery and then bring the thinner pieces down to their final sizes with the thickness planer or a handplane. For example, on a conventional table, you can mill the legs and rails first to an equal thickness, then cut your mortises and tenons. After that, send the rail pieces through the planer again to make them thinner and provide a step-back from the surface of the legs when they're joined together.

Think through the layout first I lay out the joinery dimensions for the tenons first. The tenons need to be as long as possible to maintain a strong joint. At this stage, having in hand a good sketch of the joinery detail is especially helpful.

Estimate the amount that each face will be stepped down and then experiment with different tenon sizes until you have a layout that will be strong without creating any weak areas in the joint. I leave the space between the tenons at least a little

Designing with Double-Tenon Joinery

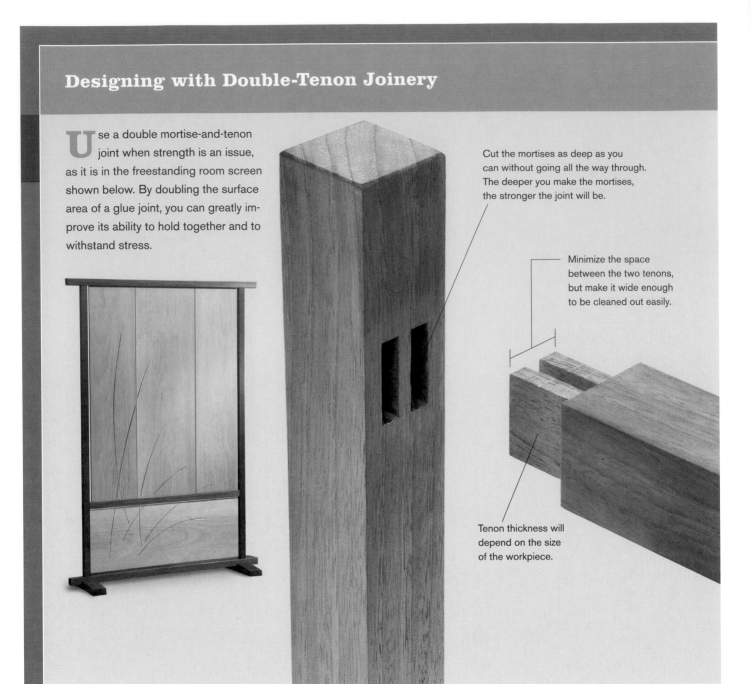

Use a double mortise-and-tenon joint when strength is an issue, as it is in the freestanding room screen shown below. By doubling the surface area of a glue joint, you can greatly improve its ability to hold together and to withstand stress.

Cut the mortises as deep as you can without going all the way through. The deeper you make the mortises, the stronger the joint will be.

Minimize the space between the two tenons, but make it wide enough to be cleaned out easily.

Tenon thickness will depend on the size of the workpiece.

wider than the narrow ⅛-in. chisel that I use to clean up that area. On the outside of both tenons, I'll often leave only a narrow shoulder, about ⅛ in. wide, which allows some leeway in deciding the thickness and spacing of the tenons.

Mark and Cut the Joinery, Starting with the Mortises

After layout, transfer the width and length of the tenons to the mortise workpieces using a marking knife. If you have to cut more than a few mortises, make a story stick from a straight scrap of wood and tack a cleat onto one end. Hook the cleat over the appropriate end of each workpiece, then transfer the mortise locations with the marking knife.

As I mentioned before, I lay out the tenons first, but when it comes time to cut the joints, the mortises come before the tenons. It's important that the two mortises line up with each other and be cut squarely. To cut mortises, I use a simple plywood-jig design based on one that Tage Frid has used.

The jig holds the workpiece in place while a four-flute center-cutting end mill mounted in a plunge router accurately cuts the mortise. The router fence simply rides against the outside of the jig. Clamp stop blocks to the jig to create mortises of identical length, and use a chisel to square up the ends of the mortises.

To fit a double mortise-and-tenon joint successfully, focus on properly fitting the outside cheeks of the tenons before dealing with the inner cheeks. Think of the first setup as fitting an extra-thick tenon into an extra-wide mortise. Chop away the wood separating the two mortises on one of the practice pieces and use this practice mortise later when you're setting up the tablesaw to cut the tenons.

Two tenons are not twice the work A tablesaw will cut the two tenons very accurately, and you can use a test piece with the tenons marked and drawn on the end of it to set up the cut.

A sliding cutoff box really helps achieve consistent results in crosscut work, and a shoulder cut along the cheeks is a good place to start. Raise the blade so that it's slightly below the pencil line representing the tenon cheek. A marking-knife tick on the side of the workpiece indicates the length of the tenon, based on the depth of the mortise. The length of the tenon should be 1/16 in. or so shorter than the depth of the mortise to ensure a snug fit and to allow room for excess glue that gets pushed into the mortise during assembly.

A stop block keeps the shoulder cut consistent as you rotate the workpiece. After you cut the first two cheek shoulders, the blade height will probably need to be changed to cut the other two sides. And here's another secret: Before cutting these two adjacent faces, put a piece of masking tape on the end of the stop block to bump away the workpiece slightly. This will keep the sawblade from nicking the previously cut shoulders.

With all four shoulders cut, clamp a straight piece of wood to the tablesaw fence. This auxiliary fence should be around 5 in. high or higher; check it with a square to ensure that it is 90 degrees to the saw table. With this setup, one hand slides along the top of the auxiliary fence, holding the workpiece firmly in position, while the other hand helps push the workpiece through the cut. Both hands are kept safely away from the blade. Set up a clean, sharp, ripping blade to cut just below the shoulder cuts. Adjust the fence to cut the practice workpiece a little proud of the outside of the tenons.

When you use this method, the waste piece falls away from the action rather than being trapped against the fence. Use a steady feed rate to move the workpiece through the cut, then rotate and cut the opposite side. Ideally, with the first pass, the tenon will be too fat to fit into the practice mortise you prepared earlier. Readjust the fence and repeat the cuts until the practice pieces go together with no sloppiness, using only hand pressure.

By fitting the outer cheeks first, there's no guessing whether it's the outer or inner cheeks that are preventing a nice fit. After you cut all the outer tenon cheeks, you can reset the fence to cut away the space between the double tenons. Sneak up on the final fit, readjusting the fence until the tenons fit nicely into a pair of mortises.

A Simple Jig for Routing Mortises

THIS JIG HAS AN IMPORTANT FEATURE. Adjustable stops on this mortising jig limit the distance the router can travel and keep the length of all of the mortises consistent.

STEADY AS SHE GOES. The router base sits firmly on the top of this jig as the router fence indexes the location of the mortise.

HELP WITH THE HANDWORK. A thick block of wood clamped firmly to the workpiece serves as a guide to chisel the ends of the mortises true and square.

Tablesawn Tenons

A HIGHER FENCE for safety and stability. The extra height of the auxiliary fence provides a firm surface to press the workpiece against and helps keep hands away from the blade. Using scraps for testing the fit, make sure the two outside cheeks fit snugly into a mortise before proceeding with the cuts for the inside cheeks.

ALMOST THERE. Tweaking the final fit requires frequent checks with the set-up scraps before you can complete the final cuts on the workpieces. A snugly fit joint will go together smoothly with moderate hand pressure.

The bandsaw makes short work of cutting the tenons to their proper width. Again, use the layout marks on your set-up pieces to determine the location of the bandsaw fence, and clamp a stop block to the fence to prevent the blade from cutting into the shoulders. Start a little wide, bumping the fence until the tenon is the same width as the squared-off mortises. Use a chisel to clean up the corners of the shoulders,

and take care to avoid damaging the adjacent shoulders. You'll need a narrow chisel to fit between the tenons and pare away the waste. To make the final assembly go more smoothly, you can use a file or a knife to cut a slight chamfer on the ends of the tenons.

CRAIG VANDALL STEVENS studied woodworking at the College of the Redwoods. Today he makes custom furniture in Sunbury, Ohio.

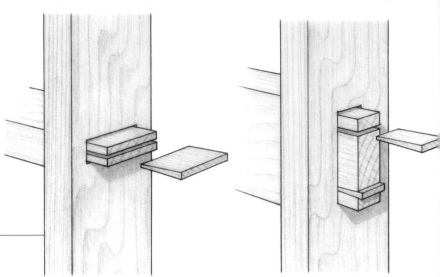

Single Fixed Wedge *Double Fixed Wedges*

The Mighty Wedge

BY JOHN NESSET

Since antiquity, wedges have served as an important means of joining wood. Low-tech but effective, they remain a useful and attractive element of joinery, evoking a rustic past when life (we like to think) was simpler and more straightforward. Like dovetails and other exposed joinery, wedges convey a sense of solid craftsmanship, even to the uninitiated.

A whole book might not be enough to detail every application for the mighty wedge, but I'll cover the two major types in their basic single and double forms. From there, furniture makers can derive other variations.

Wedges fall into two general categories: fixed and loose. Both types are driven into through-tenons to reinforce the joint. Fixed wedges generally are driven into the end grain of a tenon with glue added for reinforcement, then trimmed flush. They are appropriate where the wedge risks working loose.

Loose wedges are driven into a mortise that goes crossways through a protruding tenon. They are not glued or fastened, so they must be oriented so that gravity and/or friction will keep them in place. They are used for two reasons: to create a knock-down joint and for decorative effect.

Wedges and Grain Alignment

Whichever wedge type you choose for your project, you must take into account grain direction. The hard-and-fast rule is that a wedge must be oriented in the mortise so that it applies pressure against the grain, not across it. As young Abraham Lincoln demonstrated in his famous fence-building project, pressure applied across the grain splits the wood. In the case of fixed wedges, this fact of life will determine whether you need a single wedge or double wedges (see the drawings on p. 100).

A Single Fixed Wedge

It's worth spilling some extra ink about this first type of wedge, as it will illustrate many of the general principles for all wedged joints. For example, for any of these wedged joints, start with a carefully fitted, square mortise and tenon. For a fixed wedge (or wedges), leave the tenon just a little long, so it protrudes from the mortise ¼ in. or so.

The magic angle is 5 degrees The most important thing to know about wedges, fixed or loose, is to cut them at an angle of 5 degrees or less. In this range, friction alone will hold the wedge to the tenon. Also, if the two halves of the tenon are bent

Single Loose Wedge

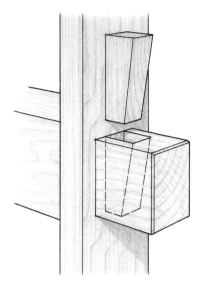

Double Loose Wedges

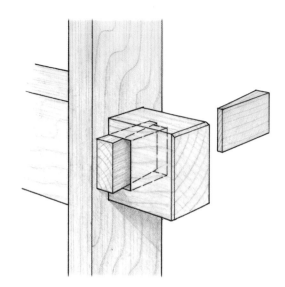

too far by a thick fixed wedge, they will be weakened at the base, thus weakening the joint.

Of course, wedges driven into the end grain of a tenon will be subjected to pressure (from racking forces and seasonal expansion and contraction) that would overwhelm friction alone, which is why the bond should be strengthened with glue.

Angle the mortise and slot the tenon

I like to cut a flare into the mortise to accommodate the wedging action, creating a dovetail of sorts and locking the joint. But often it is quite acceptable not to angle the mortise. In this case, just use a thinner wedge—cut closer to 2 degrees or 3 degrees—to increase the pressure against the sides of an already snug mortise.

A 5 degree angle works well for single fixed wedges, spreading each half of the tenon outward 2 ½ degrees (see the drawing on p. 101). The top of the mortise wall should be angled on each side to accommodate the wedging action. This offset is laid out on the edges of the mortise, on the outside face of the workpiece.

To chop the angled mortise wall, first pare away the edge of the mortise, steadily creeping back toward the scribe line and down toward the bottom edge of the mortise. The goal is to reach the line and

the bottom edge at the same time with a straight surface in between. Use the edge of the chisel to check the cut for flatness.

Next you'll want to saw a thin kerf in the tenon to receive the wedge. A handsaw leaves the right size slot. But before sawing this slot, drill a hole a little larger than the kerf through the tenon where the base of the slot should end up: about ⅛ in. from the tenon's shoulder. This hole helps prevent the tenon from splitting beyond the slot when the wedge is driven in.

Wedge basics When choosing the wood for a fixed wedge, avoid very soft species such as pine, basswood, or redwood. Instead, steer toward species such as yellow poplar, maple, and elm, which will stand up to hard pounding without splitting. Use straight-grained wood for the same reason. If you use an oily wood like ebony, clean it thoroughly with acetone immediately prior to gluing.

Cut the wedge exactly as wide as the tenon. Then lay out the appropriate wedge angle and saw it any way you like. Hand-plane it if the cut is rough. The thickness of the wedge will be determined by where you crosscut it. To allow for the wood to compress slightly, you should add a bit to the overall thickness. There is an easy way to do this: Square off the bottom of the

Orient Wedges to Avoid Splitting

A WEDGE MUST PUSH THE TENON against the end grain of the mortised piece to avoid splitting the wood. So the orientation of the tenon—along the grain or across the grain—determines the number and orientation of the wedges.

Tenons Along the Grain

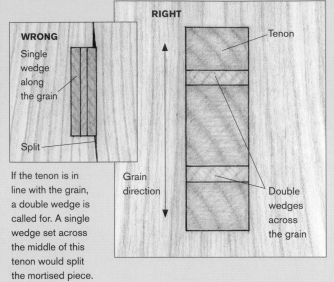

WRONG
Single wedge along the grain

Split

RIGHT

Tenon

Grain direction

Double wedges across the grain

If the tenon is in line with the grain, a double wedge is called for. A single wedge set across the middle of this tenon would split the mortised piece.

Tenons Across the Grain

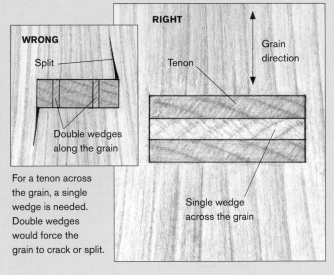

WRONG
Split

Double wedges along the grain

RIGHT

Grain direction

Tenon

Single wedge across the grain

For a tenon across the grain, a single wedge is needed. Double wedges would force the grain to crack or split.

wedge at a point where it is a hair (roughly 1/32 in.) thicker than the sawkerf.

Sharpen the squared edge to a point to make it easier to start in the slot. Then square off the thick end of the wedge at a point where it will protrude from the top of the tenon.

Driving in a wedge Assembling and gluing-up fixed-wedge joints can be nerve-wracking. I often clamp the assembly to keep the joint square and tight while the wedges are pounded home.

Do a test-run first, making sure that clamps won't come undone when you start waling away with the hammer. Drive in the

Fixed Wedges Are Glued in Place

Single Fixed Wedge

5° wedge

Offset

2½°

A 5° wedge requires each face of the mortise to be angled at 2½°. Draw a cross section of the joint to determine the amount of offset at the top of the mortise.

ANGLE THE MORTISE

LAY OUT THE OFFSET of the angled mortise. After determining the offset at the top of the mortise, scribe lines to indicate where the angled cuts begin (left). Work steadily back toward the scribe line (above) and down toward the bottom edge of the mortise.

PREPARE THE TENON FOR WEDGING

DRILL A HOLE to prevent the tenon from splitting. Clamp the workpiece vertically in a handscrew. Then drill a hole through the width of the tenon.

SAW A KERF DOWN TO THE HOLE. A handsaw leaves an appropriately narrow kerf in the tenon.

A TRICK FOR A CLEAN, FLUSH JOINT. To prevent tearout when planing a tenon flush, score a line around the base of the tenon.

Double Fixed Wedges

SOMETIMES CLAMPS ARE NEEDED. Nesset uses clamps to keep the tenon shoulders snug and square while he drives home the wedges.

3° to 4° wedge

3° to 4°

¼ in. is a good rule of thumb.

ANGLE THE ENDS OF THE MORTISE. The layout and chopping techniques are the same as when angling a mortise for a single fixed wedge.

wedge slightly to check its fit. Then pull apart the joint and apply glue to all surfaces, including some inside the sawkerf and on both faces of the wedge at its narrow end. Then insert the wedge and drive it in with a hammer. The hammering sound will change when the wedge is home, and you should see the tenon halves press tightly against the walls of the mortise.

If the wedge is wider than the head of the hammer that you're using, protect the wedge head with a block of wood as you drive it home. Be careful to hold the block square as you pound on it. When the glue dries, trim the protruding wedge and tenon flush.

Double Fixed Wedges

With a few additional considerations, the procedures for single fixed wedges apply to double fixed wedges. Like single wedges, double wedges are used in through-tenons to add strength and to give a decorative touch; double wedges are oriented across the tenon, making them much narrower.

I use a 3 degree or 4 degree angle for double wedges, which is the same amount the tenon sections will bend and the mortise wall will be angled (see the drawing on the facing page).

Basically, the wedges go in near the ends of the tenon. But exactly where to place them is a factor of how flexible the wood is. They should not be so close to the ends that the bent pieces will be weak at their base, but they should not be so close to the center that the outer pieces won't spread easily. A good rule of thumb is 1/4 in. from the end of the tenon.

Drive in the wedges equally, each a little at a time. Otherwise, the wedges will look uneven when the tenon is trimmed flush.

Loose Wedges Can Be Single or Double

As I said earlier, loose wedges offer a greater decorative effect and a sturdy knockdown joint, suitable for a trestle table, a bed frame, or the base of a workbench, among other applications.

Many of the principles that apply to fixed wedges also apply to loose ones. The 5 degree limit holds true, and the wedging action must apply pressure against the end grain of the mortised piece. However, unlike fixed wedges, which are driven in with the grain of the tenon, loose wedges are driven in perpendicularly to the grain and should be made from wood as hard or harder than the stock that they wedge to minimize compression against the end grain.

Single and double loose wedges are oriented differently. The single loose wedge generally is oriented vertically, allowing gravity to work in its favor. Double loose wedges, on the other hand, are oriented horizontally in a square mortise, wedging against each other. An occasional tap might be necessary to retighten the joint.

The familiar trestle base offers a typical application—connecting the long stretcher to the posts—for either type of loose wedge. A long, shouldered tenon at each end of the stretcher goes through the post, protruding sufficiently from the other side to accommodate a mortise for a wedge or wedges.

Start with a square, snug mortise and tenon, and a square mortise for the loose wedge(s).

Single loose wedge is vertical Single wedges, with their thick ends sticking up in plain sight, often are stylized for greater decorative effect (see the bottom drawings on p. 104).

For the single wedge, cut a square mortise vertically through the protruding tenon. Then angle the mortise face that is farthest from the post to match the wedge. I usually go with an angle of 3 degrees to 5 degrees. Cutting a taper into the wall of this long, narrow mortise is trickier than tapering the short mortises for fixed wedges, but the

Single Loose Wedge

This wedge should be oriented vertically so that gravity pulls the wedge downward when the joint wiggles, tightening it. One side of the wedge mortise is angled to match the wedge.

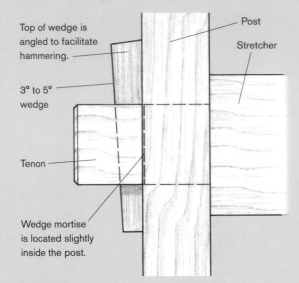

Top of wedge is angled to facilitate hammering.

Post

Stretcher

3° to 5° wedge

Tenon

Wedge mortise is located slightly inside the post.

Loose Wedges Add Style

There are many possible variations on the loose wedge, some functional, all decorative.

This wedge protects the post from the blows of a hammer.

A curved top surface protects against splitting.

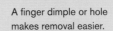

A finger dimple or hole makes removal easier.

Aesthetic variations are limitless.

ANOTHER METHOD for laying out the mortise angle. First chop a square mortise through the tenon and make the wedge stock. Insert the wedge and measure the gap at the loose end. That gap is the same amount that the mortise must be offset to match the wedge angle.

technique is the same. Lay out the offset on the wider end of the mortise, and begin removing the corner, working back toward the bottom edge and your layout line. Check the mortise wall often with a small straightedge to make sure you are keeping it straight. A mortising chisel will work better than a paring chisel, tracking along a straighter line as you chop downward.

It's important to have clean, square corners inside the wedge mortise; otherwise, the wedge will catch and could split the tenon.

Double loose wedges are another solution If the tenon is just too tall or thin for a long vertical mortise, use double loose wedges oriented horizontally. Double loose wedges work by locking against each other as well as against the mortise. One wedge

Double Loose Wedges

This type is used when the tenon is too tall to hold a long vertical wedge. The wedge mortise is horizontal and is left square because it holds two opposing wedges. Gravity won't tighten the wedges, but the mortise is easier to cut.

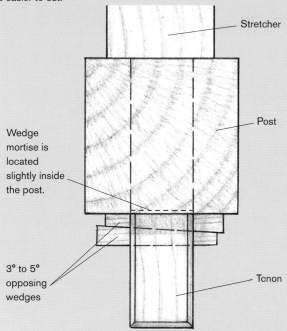

Stretcher

Post

Wedge mortise is located slightly inside the post.

3° to 5° opposing wedges

Tenon

THEN MARK THEM TO LENGTH. These wedges will end just inside the edge of the post.

TRY THE FIT, LOOKING FOR GAPS. The wedges may need light planing to adjust their fit in the mortise.

is inserted from one side and one from the other, and both are driven in until the two angled faces lock. Orientation is horizontal instead of vertical because the bottom wedge would work loose and fall out in a vertical configuration. With each edge of the wedges and the edges of their mortise neatly chamfered, the double wedge makes a useful, strong, and attractive joint.

I cut double loose wedges at a similar angle as singles, but I leave them thinner than single wedges when cutting them to length. This way, the two wedges can fit in a smaller, neater-looking mortise. Double wedges also are usually wider than single loose wedges, to offer more friction between their faces.

JOHN NESSET is a furniture maker in Minneapolis, Minnesota.

Rabbets and Dadoes

BY SVEN HANSON

Judging by the attention that dove-tails get, you'd think every craftsman cuts 200 of them a week. In reality, the rabbet, a joint with a single shoulder cut at the edge of a board, and the dado, a groove plowed inside the edge, are what many cabinetmakers use to join everyday case work.

On the evolutionary scale of joinery, the rabbet is a step above the butt joint, but it's a big step. The shoulder of a rabbet adds additional glue surface to the joint and supplies mechanical support. A dado has two shoulders, adding even more strength. The shoulders of rabbets and dadoes aid in the assembly of case work. They align the pieces when dry-fitting a case. You can check for size and fit before applying glue and clamps, which is a real boon in a one-man shop. In addition to their many applications in case work, these two joints also can be combined to produce simple but very sturdy drawers.

You can use hand tools to cut rabbbets and dadoes, but these joints are usually machined with a router or a tablesaw. Each tool has its advantages. By choosing the right tool and using a few shopmade fences and jigs, you can cut these joints accurately and quickly. The techniques are as straight-forward and uncomplicated as they are useful.

SVEN HANSON builds custom cabinetry and furniture in Albuquerque, New Mexico.

The Router Reigns for Case Work

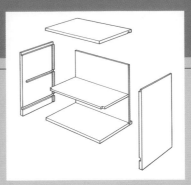

For joining the tops, sides, and backs of most case work, I prefer the rabbet joint. It's strong and simple to cut, and rabbets help with the alignment of parts during assembly. Most of the time, the rabbets go across the grain at the ends of vertical cabinet pieces (or ends of the drawer sides). I prefer using a router to cut this joint because the bit leaves a cleaner cross-grain cut than a dado blade would.

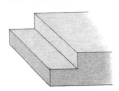

The Rabbet

Maneuvering components smoothly over a tablesaw or a router table can be difficult when building large cases. Additionally, any slight cup of the workpiece will prevent the blade or bit from cutting to its full depth. That's why I like using a hand-held router for cutting rabbets in the tops and bottoms of cases (see the photo at right). A router bit cuts cleanly and leaves a sharp, square inside corner that gives a very good surface for gluing.

ROUTER BITS WITH BEARINGS HAVE LIMITATIONS. A bearing-piloted bit (top photo) will dip into voids and round corners. The result is a sloppy rabbet (bottom photo).

A BLOCK OF WOOD and two clamps make a fence. An auxiliary fence helps create a clean rabbet by spanning dips that a bearing would follow.

Rabbeting bits come with guide bearings, but I usually remove them and guide the tool with an auxiliary fence. Bearings follow every dip in the wood, which could round the corner at the start or end of the cut (see the photos at left on the facing page).

My fence, which is nothing more than a straight block of wood clamped to the router base, provides a secure surface from start to finish, and it gives me an infinite range of adjustment. A fence also gives me the option of using straight bits to cut rabbets. When I make case goods, I usually make the depth of the rabbet half the thickness of the stock.

A cut begins with the bit well away from the work. I wiggle the router to check that the fence is snug to the edge of the board, and then I take a slow, steady pass. At the beginning of the cut, I press the front of the fence against the workpiece. Near the end of the cut, I push on the rear of the fence.

If there's no block clamped to the far side of the workpiece to combat tearout, I stop the cut an inch from the end, lift the router past the end of the board, and carefully back the cutter in to complete the cut. A second pass along the rabbet ensures a good cut.

Tall cabinets, such as entertainment centers, require internal structural support to prevent racking. Here's where I use the dado joint. A fixed shelf or panel dadoed into the sides near the center of the case adds a lot of rigidity. I cut the dadoes as deep as the corner-joint rabbets. For a snug fit, use a straight bit whose diameter matches the thickness of the panel that will be captured by the dado. If you're using sheet goods, you can order slightly under-sized bits. They come in odd sizes such as $^{23}/_{32}$ in., which is the actual thickness of most $^{3}/_{4}$-in. plywood

To guide the router, I use a shop-built T-fence (see the photos at right) clamped to the workpiece. A dado slot in the top of the fence provides a reference point for positioning the jig. When using it, I install a square base on my router. Round router bases tend to plow sawdust into the fence and then ride up on the dust

bank. I prevent tearout on the far side of the cut by clamping a backer block of hardwood where the bit will emerge.

A dado plowed right through the edge of a case side is not a pretty joint. I usually stop the dado before it comes out the front edge. Cutting a stopped dado with the T-fence and router is easy because I can see the layout marks.

The Dado

The Stopped Dado

SHOPMADE T-FENCE FOR CUTTING DADOES. Screw two strips of plywood together at right angles to make a guide fence for cutting dadoes with a router.

The Tablesaw Dominates for Drawers

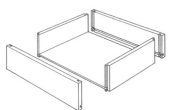

The Drawer Joint

Nothing cuts a dado faster than a tablesaw equipped with dado blades. Dado blades can be of the stack variety (see the photo below), with two outside cutters and various-sized internal chippers and shims, or wobble-style (see the photo at right), with one or two blades and a hub that allow you to dial in different settings. Stack dadoes tend to cost more but usually give you a smooth, flat-bottomed cut.

Around the time the tablesaw was invented, woodworkers figured out how to make this strong joint without the fuss and time required for dovetails. The simplified version of the drawer joint combines dadoes cut in the drawer sides with tenons cut on the front and back pieces.

Before beginning, make a custom throat plate for your tablesaw. It will reduce tearout by supporting the wood fibers on the edges of the cut. I create the opening in the plate by lowering the blades below the insert, turning on the saw, and

raising the dado blades through the insert to a predetermined height. Instead of starting and stopping the saw to measure the blade height, I mark the depth of cut on my rip fence and slowly raise the blade to that mark.

I begin this joint by first crosscutting a dado on the insides of the sides using the tablesaw's miter gauge and rip fence for guides (see photo 1). I position the dado so that when the drawer is assembled the sides will be proud of the front by just 1/32 in. That way, when you fit a false drawer front, it will fit snugly against the ends of the sides. For the drawer to end up nice and square, I make sure the rip fence is parallel to the blade and the miter gauge is square to the rip fence.

To make a matching tenon on the drawer front, I set up my saw for a rabbet cut. I set the rip fence so the dado head is partly buried in it. Because that's incompatible with hardened aluminum extrusion, I keep surplus 3/4-in. melamine-surfaced particleboard on hand for making disposable fence faces.

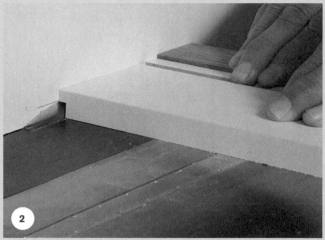

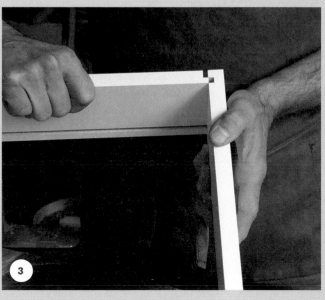

1. **CUT THE MORTISE FIRST.** Guide a drawer side against the rip fence using a miter gauge when cutting the mortise.

2. **NEXT CUT A RABBET TO CREATE A TENON.** Make this cut in a piece of scrap first, and check the fit.

3. **YOU WANT A SNUG, NOT TIGHT, FIT.** You should be able to squeeze the joint together by hand.

I set the fence so the exposed portion of the dado head equals the width of the rabbet. The exact width of the dado head doesn't matter as long as it's wider than the intended rabbet. The depth of the rabbet is set by the height of the blade. The stock is again guided by a miter gauge and a rip fence (see photo 2). It's a good idea to run some scrap stock the same size as the workpiece to check settings. The joint should be snug. If it's too tight, the short-grained sections of the mortises could break off during assembly.

Cutting Through Dovetails

BY VINCENT LAURENCE

I was trying to explain to someone years ago why I'd just taken a job as an apprentice woodworker after spending four years and $70,000 on an English degree. Suddenly, in the midst of my explanation, his eyes lit up. "You mean," he asked, "you're going to learn how to make dovetails?" He understood.

There's good reason for the lofty esteem accorded the dovetail joint. Even without glue, dovetails are very strong. And they've proven their reliability for well over three millennia. Much of their contemporary allure, though, has nothing to do with strength or reliability. Finely executed, hand-cut dovetails are a testament to the skill of the craftsman who made them.

It takes practice to cut a dovetail joint well, but the joinery is relatively simple. Two pieces of wood are connected with interlocking pins and tails. There are only two methods of cutting dovetails by hand: cutting the pins first and cutting the tails, or pin sockets, first. Both methods work. But advocates of each method tend to be passionate about the advantages of their approach and the obvious flaws in the other. Here, a pair of woodworkers with over 100 years of combined experience cutting dovetails, tells us how and why they made those choices. Their methods and tools may differ, but both cut flawless dovetails that will last generations. Here's what they had to say.

VINCENT LAURENCE is a woodworker who lives in Newtown, Connecticut.

Pins First

Tage Frid immigrated to the United States from Denmark in 1948. A furnituremaker for 50 years, he also taught woodworking for nearly four decades.

Tails First

Chris Becksvoort builds custom furniture in New Gloucester, Maine, and does restoration work for the Shaker community at Sabbathday Lake, Maine.

Tage Frid: I Cut Pins First

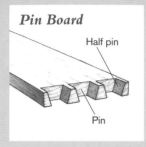

Pin Board

Half pin

Pin

I started my apprenticeship in 1928, at the age of 13. At first, I drove a push cart, delivering furniture around the city of Copenhagen. After a year, I told the master to whom I was apprenticed, "All right, I know how to drive the push cart. I'd like a bench now, so I can learn some woodworking." Within a month, I was cutting dovetails. I've cut quite a few since then and have taught hundreds of students.

Cutting the dovetail pins first makes sense. It's easier to hold the pin board in place to mark the tails than it is to hold the tail board against the end of what will be the pin board. Also, the walls of the pins provide a good surface for the awl as you mark the tails. And by marking from the inside of the joint, the angle of the pins will cause the awl to cut cleanly across the face grain of the tail board rather than follow the grain.

Another reason to cut the pins first is that when accuracy counts—when cutting the second half of the joint to fit the first—you're cutting to a line on the face grain, not on the end grain. It's easy to split this line right down the middle (but be sure the sawkerf is on the waste side of the line). Doing that in the end grain is almost impossible. It's easy to lose the line in the end grain with the first sawcut. By cutting the pins first, I don't have to worry if the saw bounces around a little on the end grain—I just cut the tails to fit.

Chris Becksvoort: I Cut Tails First

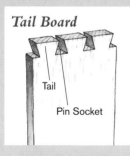

Tail Board

Tail

Pin Socket

The first time that I made dovetails, I consulted a woodworking book. It stated, in no uncertain terms, that the pins had to be cut first. Also, my father, a European-trained cabinetmaker, insisted that dovetails must be cut pins first.

But because I was a teenager with an attitude, I took these stern pronouncements as a challenge. I made the tails first, and I have been doing it that way ever since.

I find that this approach is more efficient because I can cut the tails for a pair of boards at the same time by taping them together. And because I'm not trying to match tails to pins, the cut isn't critical. When it comes time to mark the pins from the tail boards, accuracy is critical. And that's another reason I prefer cutting the tails first.

I think a knife is the most accurate tool for transferring position, more accurate than an awl and far more accurate than a pencil. But a knife will tend to follow the grain on the face of a board, which is the surface that you're marking if you use the pins to lay out the position of the tails.

When cutting the tails first, I end up marking out the pins on end grain. The knife doesn't drift or wander with the grain; it marks out the pin locations with great precision. Then I saw just outside the line and pare to the line. The result is a tight, strong, attractive joint every time.

SET THE MARKING GAUGE ¼₄ IN. WIDER than the stock, so the pins and tails will protrude slightly.

GAUGE THE BASELINE ON BOTH SIDES of both boards being dovetailed together.

MARK PINS AND HALF PINS on the end of the board. You can space them by eye, or use a ruler for more consistent spacing. A pencil mark is plenty accurate at this stage, because the pins are the first parts of the joint to be cut.

SCRIBE A BASELINE on both sides of all the boards you're dovetailing. For boards that are the same thickness, you need only one setting—the thickness of either board. When the pin board and tail board are different thicknesses, the thickness of each determines the baseline for the other.

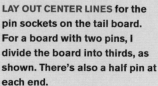

LAY OUT CENTER LINES for the pin sockets on the tail board. For a board with two pins, I divide the board into thirds, as shown. There's also a half pin at each end.

USE A CHISEL to determine the width of the pin sockets. This makes chopping the sockets much more efficient. Place the chisel over the centerline, and use a pencil to mark each side. Then mark out the half-pin sockets on the ends.

USE A BEVEL GAUGE to extend pin and half-pin marks across the end of the board. A 1:6 ratio is about the right angle for most hardwoods.

EXTEND THE PIN MARKS down to the baseline using a combination or try square.

Chris Becksvoort: I Cut Tails First continued

MARK THE ANGLES of the pin sockets with a dovetail gauge or a bevel square. Transfer these lines across the end grain. Now tape the two tail boards together, so you can cut pin sockets on both at the same time.

CUT THE TAILS. You can use a handsaw, a scroll saw, or a bandsaw with a fine blade to make cuts to the baseline. Remember to cut on the waste side of the line. Also, cut the two half-pin sockets now.

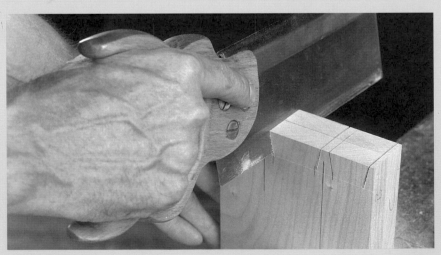

DEEPEN THE BASELINE with the corner of a chisel, and then chop a slight bevel to the baseline from the waste side. This will prevent fibers from tearing out beyond the baseline when removing the waste between pins.

CUT TO THE GAUGED BASELINE. Split the line with the sawblade on the waste side.

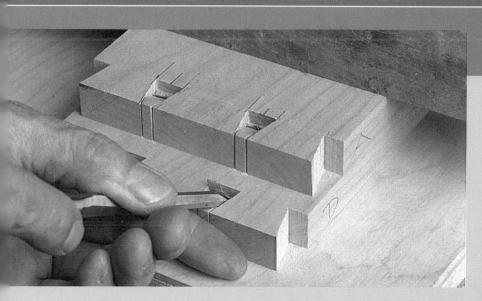

CHOP OUT THE WASTE. Start by creating a small groove on the waste side of the baseline. Then chop alternately in at a sharp angle (above) and downward at a slight angle (right). Don't chop in from the end of the board yet. Keeping the corner intact prevents tearout when the waste is removed from the center of the socket. Once you've chopped about halfway through the joint, flip the boards over and repeat. This time, though, chop from the end.

Tage Frid: I Cut Pins First continued

ALTERNATE CHOPPING from the face of the board and the end. When chopping on the face, hold the chisel in at a slight angle so that the tail slot is undercut. Chop just about halfway through the board. Flip the board over and repeat.

CONTINUE CHOPPING the board until the remaining waste drops out.

Chris Becksvoort: I Cut Tails First continued

USE A CHIP-CARVING KNIFE to clean the corners.

MARK OUT THE PINS from the tail board. Clamp the pin board into a vise, and set the tail board perpendicular to it. Make sure the edges of both boards are flush, and be sure the inside edges of all the sockets align perfectly with the inside corner of the upright board. Apply pressure to the top board, and mark the dovetails with a sharp knife (far left). Extend the pin marks down the side of the pin board using a small square. Cut down to the baseline on the waste side of the line.

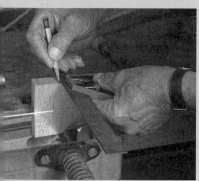

MARK THE TAILS from the pins. Hold the pin board securely in place on the tail board. The edges of both boards should be flush with each other and the inside face of the pin board should rest on the baseline of the tail board. Scribe the tail layout from the inside of the joint so that the awl follows the pins, not the grain. Extend the marks across the end of the tail board. Then cut the tails down to the baseline. A mirror makes the layout lines easier to see. Split the line on the waste side.

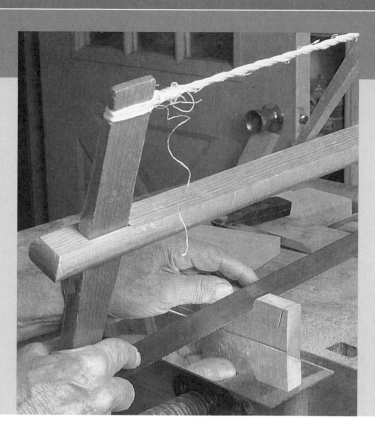

WITH AN AWL, connect the baselines from both sides of the board (left). Chop away the waste between the tails, first creating a little bevel to prevent tearout at the baseline. Alternate chopping from the end and face until you're halfway through the board (center). Then flip it over and repeat. Clean out the corners (right). The little bit of wood remaining at the base of the tails often prevents dovetails from closing.

Chris Becksvoort: I Cut Tails First continued

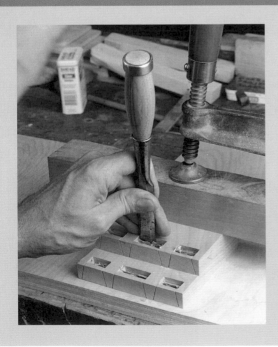

CHOP OUT WASTE BETWEEN PINS. Clamp the boards so their inside faces are up (left). This prevents the chips from becoming wedged between the pins when you finish chopping out the waste from the other side. When you're about halfway through, turn the boards over and re-clamp (center). As with the tail boards, once you've flipped the boards over, you can chop in from the end. Pare to the line with a chisel (right).

CHECK THE FIT, make any necessary corrections and tap the joint closed. It should go together with a light tap of your hand. Don't forget that the joint will swell when you apply the glue.

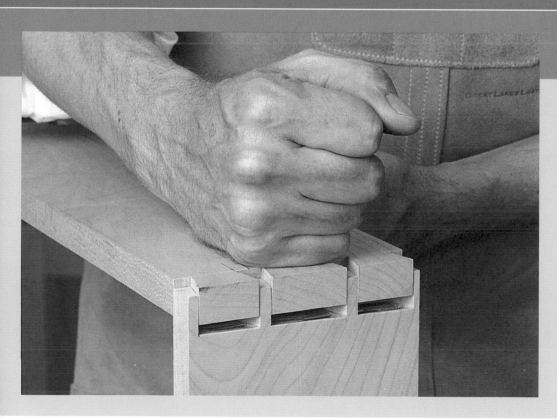

TEST-FIT THE JOINT. If you've cut and pared right up to the lines, the parts should fit like they were made for each other, a snug friction fit that comes together with a light tapping of your fist.

Housed Sliding Dovetails

BY TONY KONOVALOFF

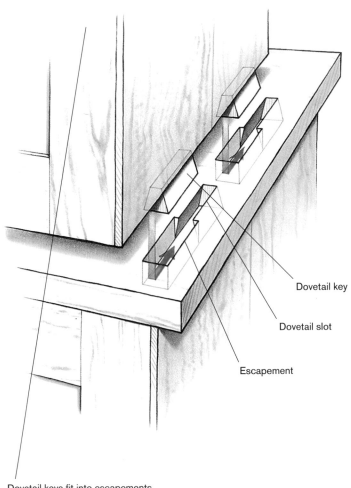

Dovetail key

Dovetail slot

Escapement

Dovetail keys fit into escapements
and slide forward into dovetail slots.

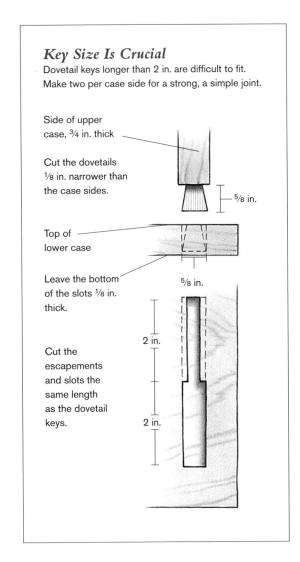

Key Size Is Crucial
Dovetail keys longer than 2 in. are difficult to fit.
Make two per case side for a strong, a simple joint.

Side of upper
case, ¾ in. thick

Cut the dovetails
⅛ in. narrower than
the case sides.

⁵⁄₈ in.

Top of
lower case

Leave the bottom
of the slots ⅛ in.
thick.

⁵⁄₈ in.

Cut the
escapements
and slots the
same length
as the dovetail
keys.

2 in.

2 in.

My shop is quite small. There is just enough room for a bench, a tool box, and a place to stand and work. I like it that way. My tools are always within easy reach and are hard to misplace. And the shop doesn't require much heat in the winter. But there's one problem: Large cabinets don't leave much room to work. Even desks take up all the available floor space. And to work on large china cabinets, I have to take down the ceiling lights.

Having a small shop doesn't keep me from making large cabinets. However, I do make a lot of knockdown joints to keep big pieces of furniture manageable.

There are endless ways to connect large case pieces, but most knockdown designs I've seen are lacking in one way or another. Some are weak; others require clunky or expensive hardware. Sliding dovetails are an option, but they show at the back of the case, and they tend to bind.

To solve some of these problems, I devised a strong connection using housed sliding dovetails (see the drawing on the facing page). I cut small dovetail keys on the bottom of the sides of the upper case and dovetail slots with escapements on the top of the lower case. The keys fit down into the escapements and then slide forward into the slots, locking the cases together and eliminating the need for hardware. And nothing shows in the front or back when the cases are assembled.

The joint holds upper and lower cases tightly together but knocks down smoothly and easily without binding. It doesn't require special tools to make or very much time. But to make sure that you understand what's going on with the joinery, it's a good idea to work up a practice piece.

Cut the Dovetails First

Before gluing up the top half of the case, I cut the dovetails on the bottoms of the case sides. There are many ways to do this.

I use a dovetail plane, but a router and jig would work as well.

Next I cut out sections of the dovetails to leave two keys, each about 2 in. long (see the photos below). The proportions of the keys depend on the thickness of the stock you use. Generally, I cut them ⅛ in. narrower than the case sides and ⅛ in. shorter than the thickness of the top of the bottom case (see the drawing detail on

AFTER CUTTING A DOVETAIL the full width of the upper case side, cope out the dovetail keys (left), and then clean up the shoulder with a chisel (below). Pare carefully: The line of the finished joint depends on the flatness of the shoulder.

Large Cases Joined Securely

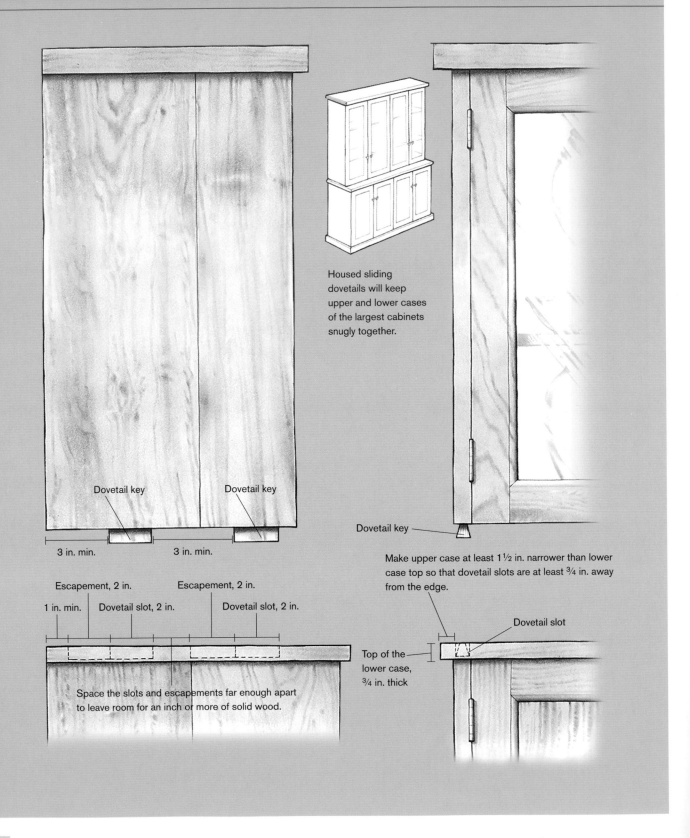

Housed sliding dovetails will keep upper and lower cases of the largest cabinets snugly together.

Dovetail key   Dovetail key

3 in. min.   3 in. min.

Escapement, 2 in.   Escapement, 2 in.

1 in. min.   Dovetail slot, 2 in.   Dovetail slot, 2 in.

Space the slots and escapements far enough apart to leave room for an inch or more of solid wood.

Dovetail key

Make upper case at least 1½ in. narrower than lower case top so that dovetail slots are at least ¾ in. away from the edge.

Dovetail slot

Top of the lower case, ¾ in. thick

MARK THE DOVETAIL SLOTS
FIRST.
**The locations for dove-
tail slots in the top of the lower
cabinet are marked directly
from the dovetailed keys.**

p. 122). Their placement is important. They
must be far enough apart so they don't interfere with each other. If the dovetails are
2 in. long, the escapements and slots must
each be 2 in. long. To maintain strength,
each slot and escapement pair should be
at least an inch apart. This means that 2-in.
dovetails must be spaced at least 3 in. apart,
and the front of the rear dovetail must be
3 in. from the back of the upper case.

After I cut the keys to length, I complete the upper case. It's important to remember that the shoulders of the dovetail
keys rest on the top of the lower case. Only
the keys should extend below the line of
the shoulders; otherwise, the upper case will
not sit evenly on the lower case, and the
joint will not function properly.

Lay Out the Dovetail
Slots and Escapements

Once the upper case has been glued and assembled, I can lay out the escapements and
dovetail slots on the top of the lower case.
I start by placing the upper case onto the

**LAYOUT THE ESCAPEMENTS
using the dovetail slots as a
guide. When you cut the joints,
remember that the escapements
are at the back of the cabinet.**

lower case and marking the front, back, and
sides of each slot and escapement. To determine the width of the top of the dovetail
slots, I transfer the measurement from the
dovetails themselves with vernier calipers
(see the photos on p. 126). It is important
that the upper case be assembled: It's the

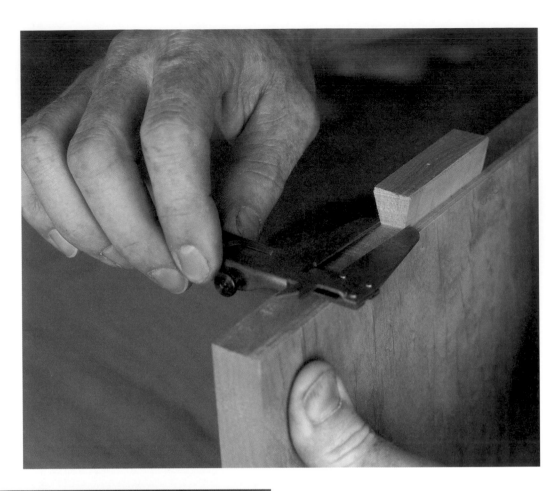

DON'T MEASURE, TRANSFER.
The tops of the dovetails and slots should be the same width. Find the width with a vernier caliper (right), and then mark it in the middle of the slot (bottom).

only way to be absolutely sure the slots will be in the right place. However, this isn't necessary when making a practice piece.

Cut the Escapements Before the Dovetail Slots

I remove the bulk of the waste from the escapements with a brace and bit and pare to the lines with a chisel. I cut them just slightly deeper than the dovetails are tall. You don't need to leave as much stock in the bottom of the escapements as you would for a sliding dovetail, just enough to keep them solid. I leave about ⅛ in. of material at the bottom of each. I test-fit the dovetails in the escapements before I cut the dovetail slots. The dovetails should just slip into the escapements with no extra room front or back. The shoulders of the dovetails, not the bottoms of the escapements, hold the weight of the upper case.

CAREFULLY PARE THE SLOT WALLS. Cut a little at a time, and test the fit frequently. Pay attention to the angle. It's easy to wander from it.

JUST PULL BACK, AND LIFT OUT. The housed sliding dovetail requires no contortions to take apart, even though it is very solid when assembled.

Fit the Slots to the Dovetails

I cut the slots slightly undersized and then pare them to fit the dovetails bit by bit. I work slowly, keeping an eye on the angle and the marked lines. The hard part is that you can't really see what you are trying to fit. Don't try to get it all at once (see the top photo above).

Fitting the first ¼ in. or so of each dovetail makes a good reference for cutting the rest of the slots. The finished joint should feel snug, neither binding nor loose. Putting it together and taking it apart shouldn't take a mallet or Herculean strength.

After you've finished the joint, apply a good coat of paste wax to all parts of the dovetails and slots. The wax helps the joint work smoothly. You now have a hidden, stable, and graceful knockdown connection for a two-piece cabinet.

TONY KONOVALOFF is a professional furniture maker in Oak Harbor, Washington.

Pinned Box Joints

BY SETH JANOFSKY

SIMPLE ELEGANCE. Square, broad tabs interlock at the corners of solid-wood cases and boxes, such as this *tansu*-style chest-on-chest. Because of the lack of long-grain gluing surface, each tab is pinned to add mechanical strength.

Boxes are the essential structure of all case pieces. That means a large part of furniture making boils down to joining pieces of wood to make boxes. There are many ways of doing this. Some, such as dovetails, draw attention to the joinery and the box structure itself, while others, such as post-and-panel construction, hide those aspects.

Enter the box joint, a close cousin of the dovetail that also becomes part of the overall look of a piece. Like the dovetail, the box joint is a way of solidly joining two planks or panels of solid wood end-to-end, appropriate for anything from jewelry boxes to full-size cabinet components. In essence, the box joint involves making a number of interlocking fingers on the ends of the pieces to be joined. The more well-known variety of the box joint, which I call a finger joint, has many small inter-

locking fingers. The fingers provide plenty of long-grain-to-long-grain gluing surface. The version I introduce here, however, has relatively broad fingers and must be pinned to add mechanical strength.

The pinned box joint is common in some traditional types of furniture, such as Japanese solid-carcase construction (*tansu*) and also the Craftsman work it inspired in this country, most notably that of Charles and Henry Greene. The pinned box joint also can be used to give an Asian flavor to contemporary work. There are a couple of attractive variations on this joint (see the drawings below). One is a dovetailed version, which also is seen in *tansu* furniture. Another is the Greene-and-Greene version, which has longer fingers that protrude slightly.

To me, the pinned box joint, with its large fingers, is most suitable for large boxes

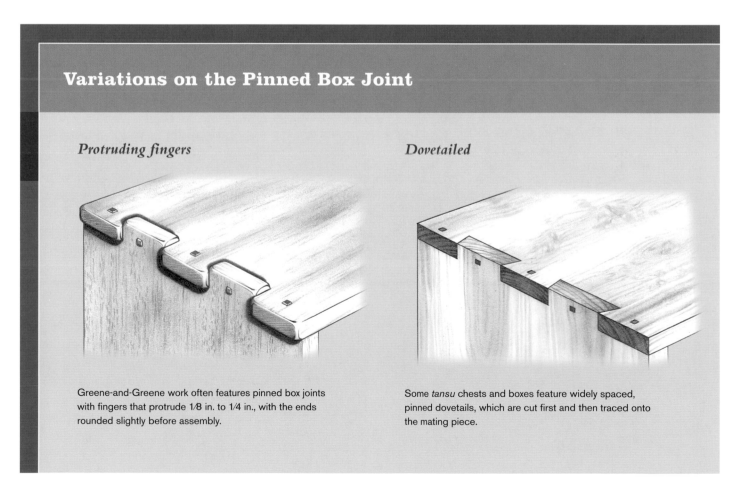

Variations on the Pinned Box Joint

Protruding fingers

Greene-and-Greene work often features pinned box joints with fingers that protrude 1/8 in. to 1/4 in., with the ends rounded slightly before assembly.

Dovetailed

Some *tansu* chests and boxes feature widely spaced, pinned dovetails, which are cut first and then traced onto the mating piece.

Design and Layout

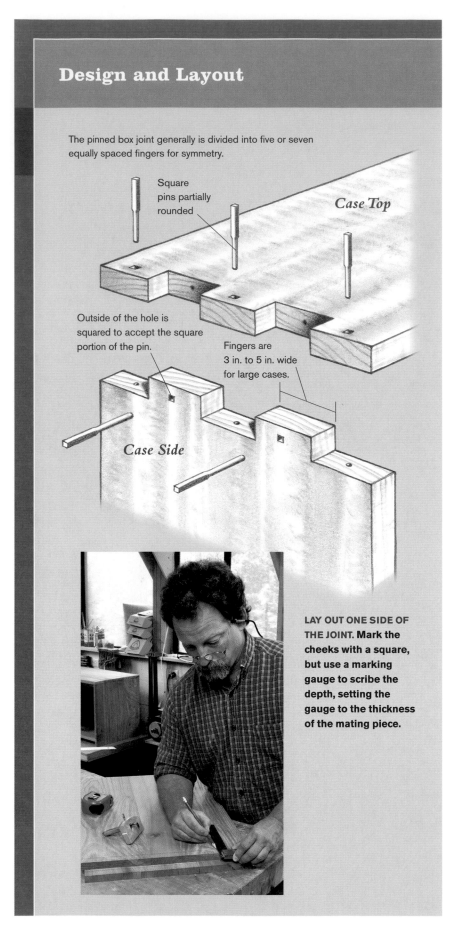

The pinned box joint generally is divided into five or seven equally spaced fingers for symmetry.

Square pins partially rounded

Case Top

Outside of the hole is squared to accept the square portion of the pin.

Fingers are 3 in. to 5 in. wide for large cases.

Case Side

LAY OUT ONE SIDE OF THE JOINT. Mark the cheeks with a square, but use a marking gauge to scribe the depth, setting the gauge to the thickness of the mating piece.

and full-size carcases such as blanket chests. I think of finger joints as being more appropriate for small boxes, trays, and the like.

Cutting the Joint

Box joints can be cut by machine, by hand, or as I like to do it, by both. I think it is easiest to cut these large joints in the same manner as hand-cut dovetails; that is, by clamping the workpieces vertically to the bench and sawing down the layout lines with a handsaw. As with a dovetail joint, it's best to cut one half of the box joint, transfer the lines to the other part, and then cut it to match.

On this joint, as on dovetails, I saw right to the layout lines because I think doing so is easier than trying to pare the joint to fit. Next, I remove most of the waste between the sawcuts with a jigsaw or bandsaw. I generally find it easiest to finish the cuts with a dado set on the tablesaw, working right to the sawkerfs and scribe line. This works well unless the pieces are very large and unwieldy. In such cases, I clean up with a router (see the photos on the facing page).

Once the joints have been cut, glue-up is straightforward, but you need to remember all of the basic stuff: to cut whatever grooves are needed for bottoms or backs beforehand (through-grooves on one set of parts, stopped grooves on the other); to finish the insides of the parts before assembly, if it's appropriate to the project; and to do a dry-fit to ensure that everything goes together tightly and squarely.

Reinforcing the Joint with Pins

The first thing I do is mill the stock for the pins. I consider the wood for the pins rather carefully. On the one hand, I want a wood that harmonizes well with the wood of the carcase, neither too close nor too far away in tone. In general, I look for enough contrast to be distinct, yet not look flamboyant

Cut the Fingers

Cut one side of each joint, then transfer the layout to the other side. Use a handsaw to make precise cuts where the fingers join.

SAW THE CHEEKS and chop out most of the waste. Janofsky uses a Japanese dovetail saw (left), which cuts on the pull stroke and should be held at the end of its handle for the best results. Cut right to the layout lines, being careful to keep the cut straight and square. Use a bandsaw or jigsaw (above) to remove most of the waste.

TWO WAYS TO FINISH THE JOB

Depending on the size of the workpieces, the rest of the waste can be removed either on the tablesaw or with a router. Cut right to the sawkerfs and scribe line.

A TABLESAW SLED will handle shorter pieces. Adjust a dado set to cut to the scribe line. Use a sacrificial fence to minimize chipout on the back side of the cut.

TALL PIECES ARE EASIER to handle with a router. Clamp pieces in pairs to give the router a wider bearing surface. Set the bit depth right to the scribe mark.

TRANSFER THE LAYOUT to the mating piece. Align the pieces carefully and make small tick marks. Then use a square to carry those marks around the mating workpiece.

Peg the Joints

Be sure to drill the pinholes straight (below). Then square off the top section for the square pins.

SHOPMADE TOOL for squaring holes. Janofsky uses a thin, square bar of steel, tapered on a bench grinder, to square the holes. The wood block makes the tool easier to hold.

or call too much attention to itself. Also, the wood for the pins usually should be darker, not lighter, than the background wood. Often I end up using white oak for the pins. The Greene brothers favored ebony, but for me this is too strong a statement. In traditional *tansu*, Japanese furniture makers typically used *utsugi*, which is described as being somewhat similar to dogwood.

Functionally, the important thing is to choose a wood that is quite strong—after all, the point is to add strength to the joint. Also, the pins get hammered in with a fair amount of force.

Once I have milled strips of the stock for the pins, I drill holes through the parts of the joint from the outside, being careful to drill straight. Generally, I use pins between ⅛ in. and ¼ in. thick, depending on the thickness of the case pieces and the overall look of the piece.

Usually I prefer square pins, but this again is a matter of taste. Whether they're round or square, I leave the pins extralong by an identifiable amount (say, ½ in.) to allow for pounding. The extra length also lets me see when the pins have penetrated the joint to the proper depth. If round, the pins need to be whittled or shaved,

DRIVE HOME THE PINS. Add give to the pin and hole, and drive in each pin while holding it in alignment with a wrench.

WHITTLE THE PINS. The pins start off square, sized to fit the top of the hole and roughly ½ in. extralong. Then all but the top 1 in. is whittled round (left).

TRIM AND PLANE the joint flush (below). Use a flush-cutting saw to trim the pins, then plane and/or sand the surfaces flush.

ideally in such a way that they are slightly too small at the inner ends and a bit too large at the outer ends.

If the pins are to be square, I whittle each pin almost round as described above but leave the outer portion square. My secret to a nicely defined pin is to square the outer part of each hole, too, by pounding into it a tapered piece of steel before installing the pins (see the right photo on the facing page).

I fill all of the holes with glue and smear some on each pin for good measure. Then I pound the pins into the holes, hammering them down hard, but not so hard that the pins break or the carcase wood splits.

Remember that the primary purpose is to strengthen the joint, so success is a matter of sizing the holes and the pins appropriately. Practice makes perfect.

When the glue is dry, I trim the pins and level the entire joint. Usually, a hand-plane is enough, but sometimes I pull out the belt sander for more serious stock removal.

And there you have it: a beautiful and strong joint you can be proud of, with a truly distinctive look.

SETH JANOFSKY is a furniture maker in Fort Bragg, California.

Shopmade
Slot Mortiser

BY GREGORY PAOLINI

As a member of a professional guild, I make a lot of Arts and Crafts style furniture, and I cut countless mortise-and-tenon joints. I used to cut the joints with a combination of hand and power tools, but I quickly realized that I had to find a more efficient way if I was going to keep the price of my furniture out of the stratosphere. I tried many different methods, but when I saw furniture maker and teacher Gary Rogowski using a slot mortiser, I was sold on the idea.

A slot mortiser basically is a table with a horizontally mounted router equipped with a spiral bit. The mortise is cut by plunging the workpiece into the bit while moving the workpiece from side to side to bore its width. Slot mortisers are the choice of production shops because they are very fast, accurate, and work well with integral or loose tenons.

I went shopping for a slot mortiser and found some machines that could do everything I needed—except fit into my budget. Prices for joint-making machines and commercial slot mortisers ranged from about $450 to $2,600★, and in some cases I still had to supply my own router. Talk about sticker shock. I figured, for that much money, why not try to make my own.

Like the commercial machines, mine had to be reliable and accurate. It needed to incorporate a horizontally mounted router, a table that could move on both X and Y axes, stops to control mortise width and depth, and a system to index and secure my work.

Build Heavy Sliding Tables from MDF

Building the movable table was the tricky part. I needed a system that would provide movement independently along two axes. I achieved the X-Y movement I was after by making two platforms, each of which moves along a different axis, with aluminum T-tracks riding in dadoes. The table also had to be stable and strong, as well as a little weighty, to resist jumping or jerking when cutting. Three stacked layers of ¾-in.-thick medium-density fiberboard (MDF) provided both the weight and the stability I needed.

T-tracks make great runners for jigs. They fit into a dado that is ¾ in. wide. They don't swell and shrink like hardwood runners. And you can bolt things onto them—in this case, I bolted a couple of MDF blocks that act as stops to limit platform travel in each direction. Additionally, the T-track I used can accept standard ¼-in. by 20-tpi bolts, which keeps hardware and fastener costs to a minimum. Some brands of T-tracks require you to buy specialty hardware.

Keep T-Tracks Aligned

It is important that the upper (X) and lower (Y) sliding platforms move perpendicular and parallel, respectively, to the cutting bit. To ensure this, I cut all of the matching T-track dadoes at the same time with the same settings on the tablesaw. For instance, two ⅛-in.-deep dadoes in the underside of the X platform along its length were cut at the same time as the matching dadoes in the top side of the Y platform below. As a result, T-tracks mounted in the dadoes on the Y platform are aligned perfectly with the dadoes above.

The T-tracks on the base of the slot mortiser are screwed to the surface, so no dadoes are required. However, those T-tracks fit into dadoes cut in the underside of the Y platform along its width. Once the T-tracks are installed, applying a little furniture wax cuts down on wear to the MDF platforms and helps the mortiser work smoothly.

To finish the X platform, I cut a series of dadoes in the top surface for two more T-tracks, on which I can mount index blocks that act as a fence to butt a workpiece against.

Simple-to-Make Mortiser

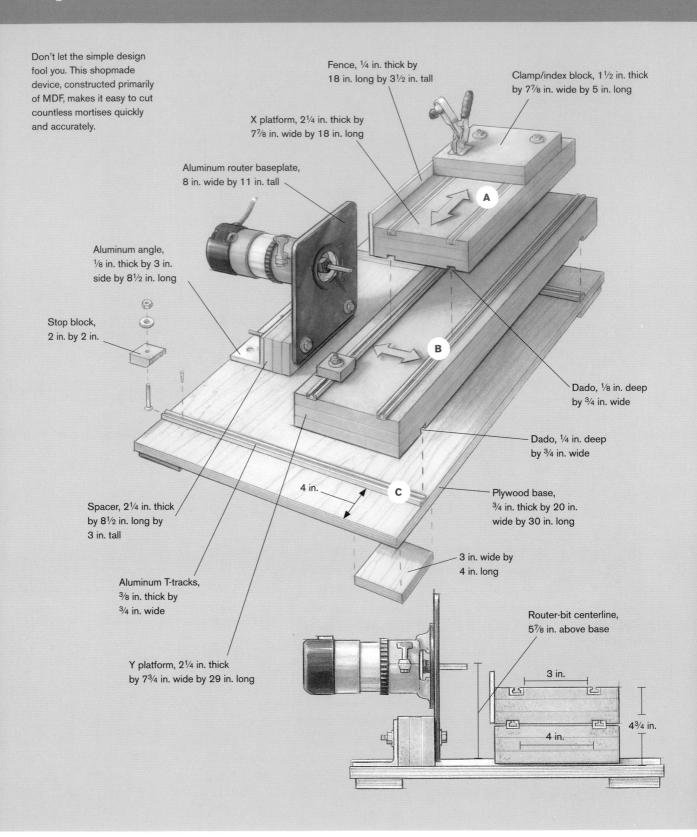

Don't let the simple design fool you. This shopmade device, constructed primarily of MDF, makes it easy to cut countless mortises quickly and accurately.

Fence, 1/4 in. thick by 18 in. long by 3 1/2 in. tall

Clamp/index block, 1 1/2 in. thick by 7 7/8 in. wide by 5 in. long

X platform, 2 1/4 in. thick by 7 7/8 in. wide by 18 in. long

Aluminum router baseplate, 8 in. wide by 11 in. tall

Aluminum angle, 1/8 in. thick by 3 in. side by 8 1/2 in. long

Stop block, 2 in. by 2 in.

A

B

Dado, 1/8 in. deep by 3/4 in. wide

Dado, 1/4 in. deep by 3/4 in. wide

4 in.

C

Plywood base, 3/4 in. thick by 20 in. wide by 30 in. long

Spacer, 2 1/4 in. thick by 8 1/2 in. long by 3 in. tall

3 in. wide by 4 in. long

Aluminum T-tracks, 3/8 in. thick by 3/4 in. wide

Router-bit centerline, 5 7/8 in. above base

Y platform, 2 1/4 in. thick by 7 3/4 in. wide by 29 in. long

3 in.

4 in.

4 3/4 in.

T-Tracks Are the Key to Smooth Operation

THE MOVABLE PLATFORMS don't make contact with one another; instead, they slide solely on the aluminum T-tracks. The tracks also secure the clamping blocks. Wax the tracks regularly to ensure smooth movement.

A. T-tracks that secure the clamping blocks are fully recessed into the X platform.

⅛ in.

B. T-tracks that support the X platform are partially recessed into the Y platform.

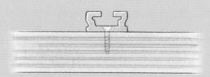

C. T-tracks that support the Y platform are surface-mounted to the plywood base.

Mount the Router on a Baseplate

Keeping the router from deflecting while in use is critical, and I didn't think that a plastic router base was up to the task. Instead, I attached the router to a standard aluminum router baseplate and made a spacer from MDF and a piece of ⅛-in.-thick by 3-in. by 3-in. aluminum angle to secure the baseplate to the table base. When securing the router plate to the aluminum angle, make sure the router-bit centerline is 5⅞ in. above the base. This is an ideal height for cutting mortises into most furniture parts.

Also, it's important to reference the router baseplate against the X and Y platforms with a square while securing it to the base. This will ensure that the mortises are cut at a perfect 90 degrees.

Use spacers to adjust the height of a mortise—Unlike commercial machines, the bit on this slot mortiser can't be adjusted for the height of a mortise. Instead, I raise or lower the workpiece with spacers of various thicknesses. For example, to cut a ¼-in. mortise in the center of a ¾-in.-thick workpiece, I use a ¾-in. spacer.

It takes some fooling around to determine spacer thickness, but once you have made a few spacers for various projects, label and save them for future use. I also have angled spacers that allow me to cut angled mortises, expanding the versatility of the tool. You can fine-tune the height with plastic laminate or cardstock shims.

Cutting Mortises for a Leg-to-Apron Joint

The slot mortiser works well for cutting mortises into two mating pieces to be joined with a loose tenon. And the mortiser can be adjusted quickly to cut a multitude of mortises.

SET UP THE APRON MORTISE FIRST

ADJUST MORTISE DEPTH ON THE ROUTER. The distance from the fence to the end of the router bit determines the depth of the mortise (top left).

CLAMP THE APRON to the sliding platforms. Set the mortise height with a spacer. Then butt the workpiece against the fence and index block, and clamp it in place (above).

ADJUST THE STOP BLOCKS TO THE CORRECT MORTISE WIDTH. Align the router bit with one end of the mortise, butt the stop block against the sliding platform, and secure it in place (left).

Using the Slot Mortiser

Lay out the first mortise in a series with a marking gauge, and then set up the slot mortiser. Verify that the mortise height is correct and that the stop blocks are set accurately (see the photos above).

Once you've cut the first mortise, you can use most of the settings to cut the mating mortise. Finally, the two pieces can be joined with a loose tenon, cut from the same material and planed to fit the mortises.

★ Price estimates are from 2005.

GREGORY PAOLINI makes Arts and Crafts style furniture at his home in Depew, New York.

Mortise the Aprons

Apply light pressure against the bit and move the workpiece side to side, cutting deeper with each pass.

Stop blocks on the Y platform limit the mortise width.

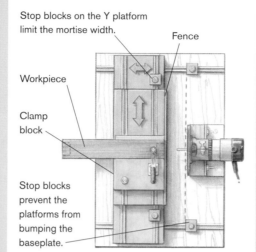

Fence

Workpiece

Clamp block

Stop blocks prevent the platforms from bumping the baseplate.

Mortise the Legs

The clamp block is used as an index block to register the end of the leg. A second clamp block is added to secure the leg.

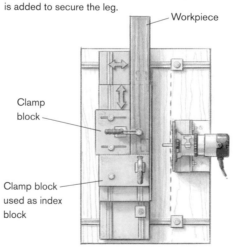

Workpiece

Clamp block

Clamp block used as index block

Sources

Brunner Enterprises
877-299-2622;
T-tracks
www.brunnerent.com

Rockler
800-279-4441;
Router BasePlate
www.rockler.com

Joint-Making Machines

BY MICHAEL STANDISH

Compared with more fundamental equipment such as jointers, mortise-and-tenon machines, or jigs, are woodshop luxuries. They can feature ingenious and sophisticated designs, but in the end, like dovetail jigs, they are adjuncts to routers. Jigs are not cheap either: The models surveyed here are priced from a little over $400 to about $700★, router not included. With some forethought and care in the making, serviceable shopmade versions are fairly straightforward and inexpensive to construct. So why buy a factory-made one?

A proper jig serves two basic woodworking functions: securing a workpiece and guiding a cutter. The jig should perform without surprises and without fail. Also, a jig should enhance the advantages of machine joinery by adding control (and thus precision) and speed to the process. The jigs in this article meet all of these demands, allowing you to cut a mortise-and-tenon joint in the time it takes to hone a chisel. Although some of them also feature ways to cut other joints (through-, half-blind, and sliding dovetails; box joints; dadoes; fancy pin-and-crescent joints), for this review I wanted to learn only how well the jigs could cut basic mortise-and-tenons—the most commonly used joint in furniture and cabinetry.

The makers of these machines have already done much of the head-scratching for you (How to center the cut? Will the clamps interfere? Is the router adequately supported?). The streamlined clamping arrangements of these very different designs drastically reduce stock-handling hassles, and their refined adjustment mechanisms allow precisely and predictably fitted joints.

All of these jigs will require an hour or longer for assembly, and you'll need several times that to familiarize yourself with how

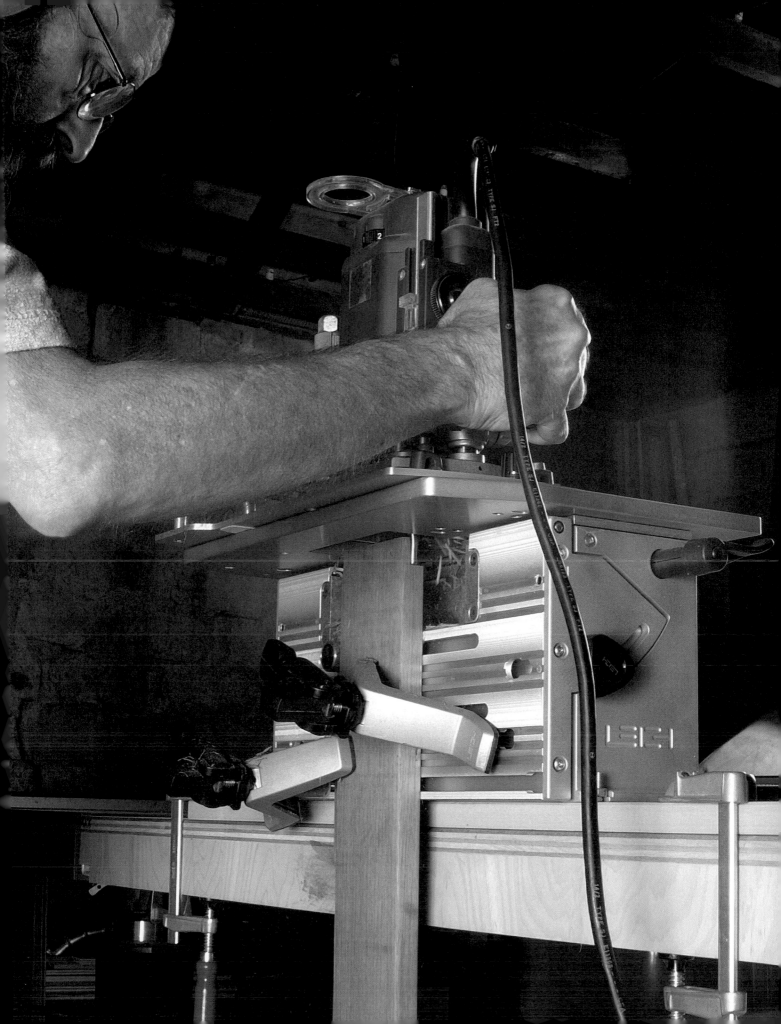

Leigh® FMT Jig

Price: $689

Source: www.leevalley.com

800-663-8932

The FMT in the name stands for frame mortise and tenon, and this machine was specifically designed for making these joints. Leigh's pin-and-template guide system is as close to foolproof as I can imagine anyone could make it. The auxiliary baseplate has two tapered pilot pins that engage slots in a template for mortising, and they ride the perimeter of the same template to mill matching tenons. Raising or lowering the pins alters the fit of the joint in repeatable 0.001-in. increments. Templates provided with the standard unit allow for more than 20 sizes of mortise-and-tenon joints; additional guides are available individually or in sets, which will give you up to 50 different sizes of joints to cut. For angled work, such as that often found in chairs, the clamping plate can be swiveled up to a setting of 30°.

At about 18 in. wide by 12 in. deep by 9 in. high, the Leigh jig is compact to the point of being portable, and its looks—sporting an exceptional level of finish and engineering—are not deceiving. In operation, this jig was exceptionally smooth and precise. Also, the owner's manual was refreshingly comprehensive, clear, and concise.

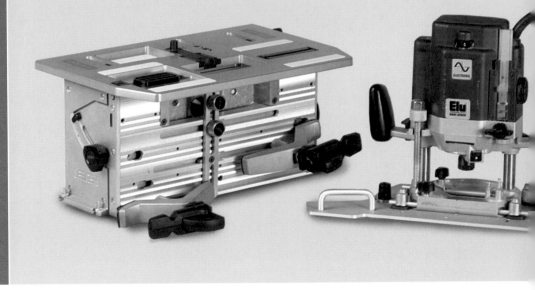

they work. Some particular operations, such as cutting the joints for a set of different-size cabinet doors, will entail additional time for individual setups. Regardless of your woodworking style or mechanical aptitude, the latter prep work typically is measured in minutes, while the machining itself takes even less time. Results, of course, will vary. But with a good router and a sharp bit, you reasonably can expect to produce between one and four consistently crisp mortises or tenons per minute with any of these jigs.

Testing Procedures

I tested these jigs with a 15-amp Elu™ plunge router, run at the same speed setting, using the same solid-carbide spiral upcut

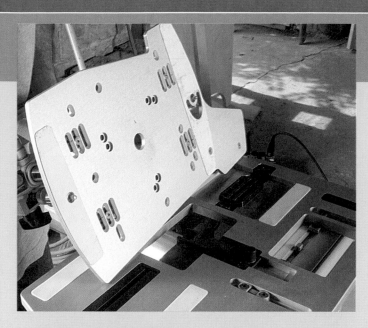

GUIDANCE SYSTEM IS FINELY TUNED. Visible on the left and right of the underside of the baseplate are the two tapered pins that engage grooves in the two black plastic inserts fitted into the top of the table. By changing the inserts you can cut various sizes of matching mortises and tenons.

ALIGN THE WORKPIECE. Scribe pencil lines on the workpiece at the centerline of the joint. Align them with crosshairs on the sliding black plastic alignment gauge.

SECURE THE WORKPIECE. Two cam clamps accommodate any thickness up to 3 in. and any width up to 5 in. The stock length is limited by how high the jig is mounted off the floor.

bit. I machined mortises and single tenons, approximately 1 in. by 3 in. in profile, with all of these jigs. Material for the test samples came from the same bundle of mahogany-like substitute decking purchased from a local lumberyard. I tested these machines by cutting roughly two dozen mortises and two dozen tenons on each of them.

I then measured the results with a dial caliper. Manufacturers of polyvinyl acetate adhesives (most conventional white and yellow glues) usually recommend tolerances within 0.005 in. for optimum performance. Shooting for this level of accuracy may seem pretty ambitious, but attaining such precision goes a long way toward justifying the use (and, not incidentally, the purchase)

MatchMaker®

Price: $699

Source: www.woodworker.com

800-645-9292

Mortising with the MatchMaker will be familiar to anyone who's ever used an industrial-level horizontal mortising machine. The design is similar to that of the JDS Multi-Router® (see p. 148). For mortises, the workpiece carriage is levered in and out and left to right along roller bearings on guide rods, moving against a router that is mounted horizontally in a fixed position. For these X and Y axes movements, you can use a simple tapered handle or a pivoting joystick, depending upon the range of motion required to cut a given joint. The tapered handle provides a larger range of motion.

For tenons, the router carriage is freed so that its integral stylus, or guide pin, can bear against a template, and the router is moved up and down on a Z axis with a

sturdy, pivoting handlebar. The operation is like a cross between a duplicating lathe and a pantograph, and although it takes a bit of getting used to, it's more complicated in the telling than in the milling. The tenon templates are made to be 0.003 in. to 0.005 in. smaller than their nominal size. The manufacturer (Woodtek®) recommends fine-tuning the fit of the joint by wrapping one or two layers of cellophane tape around the stylus.

The MatchMaker is the only jig that I surveyed that mills tenons with the workpiece oriented horizontally. As a result, it will accommodate long workpieces, such as bed rails and aprons for large dining tables, without the operator having to modify or adapt the machine in any way.

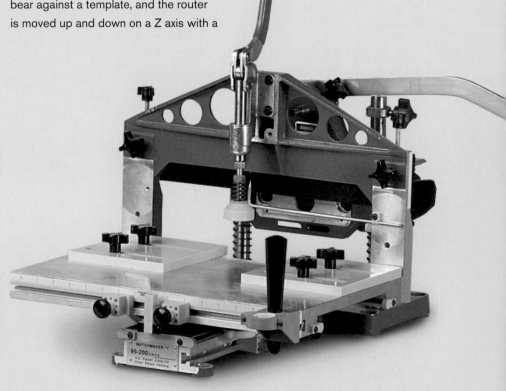

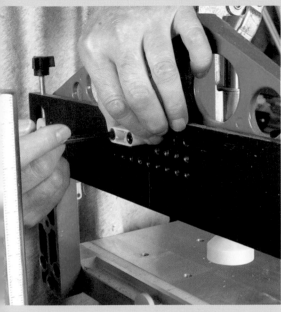

SECURE A TEMPLATE TO CUT A TENON. The yellow plastic template is fastened into threaded holes in the yoke assembly with two Allen-head screws.

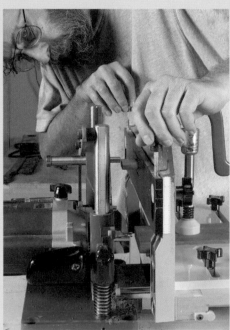

LOCATE THE TENON CUT. Vertical adjustments in the yoke assembly will affect where a tenon is cut on the workpiece. The steel stylus shown here is mounted at a fixed distance from the cutter, and you can use either the small or large end of the stylus to follow the template, which affects the size of the cut.

CENTER THE WORKPIECE ON THE SLIDING TABLE. A toggle clamp holds the workpiece tight to the sliding table, and two yellow plastic plates bear against the edges of the workpiece to prevent any lateral movement.

QuickTenon

Price: $418

Source: www.quicktenon.com;
301-746-8092

In the midst of handsomely finished, powder-coated or anodized-metal, and precision high-tech plastic extrusions, stands the modest-looking QuickTenon. Bare bones it is, but in the best sense. It is essentially a freestanding plywood table with a built-in side vise and a sliding phenolic plate. A router-mounted collar guide tracks against the center slot of this plate, whose left-to-right travel is limited by adjustable stop blocks. Placing shim stock (or an automotive feeler gauge) between block and plate makes for simple, accurate, and virtually instantaneous adjustments. This fixture also is designed to mill dovetails, such as for a table's apron-to-leg joints, and flipping a small subplate allows you to change from making the usual round-end tenons—matching the profile of its router-bored mortises—to square ones, such as you'd want for through-tenon work.

ADJUST THE PLATE TO CENTER THE CUT. The phenolic plate rides left to right on four loose bearings that rest on the plywood tabletop and is held in place by the two aluminum bars on both ends.

ROUND OR SQUARE TENONS. By varying the shape of the adjustable inserts in the phenolic plate, you can cut either round or square tenons.

BUILT-IN VISE HOLDS THE WORKPIECE IN PLACE. The crank (at left in photo) controls a plywood box that pushes against the workpiece to hold it secure. The top surface of the workpiece should be flush with the top of the plywood table.

of one of these jigs, even for relatively small-scale production work. The majority of all of the test samples measured within 0.002 in. of their intended dimensions—well within the tolerances recommended by adhesive manufacturers.

The Choice Is Not Only Budget-Driven

In a survey like this, it's customary to choose a winner, but on this score I feel a bit like a bus driver sent to test Ferraris against Porsches. For machine joinery, all of these jigs are impressively precise and

WoodRat

Price: $545

Source: www.woodrat.com;
866-966-3728

Although you can make a stand for this fixture, the recommended wall-mounting (the manual provides details) is better because it's simpler, sturdier, and saves floor space. Unique to the WoodRat is a power feeder that moves the workpiece side to side against the router bit, which is mounted vertically overhead. Although the power feeder is a hand-cranked system, it's a smooth and sure way of climb cutting. Workpieces are held in place against an aluminum angle by a locking cam lever that slides along a slotted track. The slotted track, aluminum stop, and brass gauge blocks and spacers all speed up the setup time required for making joints with this jig. An overhead plunge router is mounted to a sliding plate that can be moved front to back.

The WoodRat produces square-edged tenons and rounded mortises, so you'll have to either round off the corners of the tenons by hand or chisel out the mortises to get matching profiles in the finished joint.

The manufacturer also offers a smaller version of this jig, called the LittleRat, with similar but more limited cutting capacities. It's available for about 40 percent less money, but the sizes of the workpieces you can process with it are smaller.

CAM CLAMP HOLDS THE STOCK IN PLACE. A cam clamp slides along a slotted track and presses the workpiece against a sturdy piece of aluminum angle.

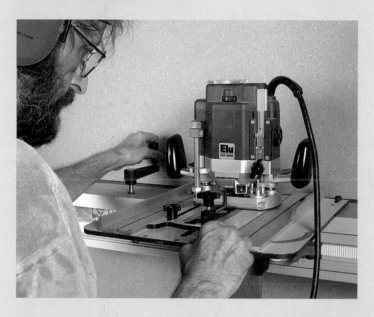

CLIMB CUTS ARE CLEANER. You can virtually solve the problem of chipout on the leading edge of the router cut by moving the workpiece in a clockwise direction around the cutter.

almost laughably fast once you overcome the initial learning curve.

The Leigh (p. 142) and the QuickTenon (facing page) are faster in setting up, fine-tuning, and machining mortise-and-tenon joints. The MatchMaker (p. 144) and the WoodRat (above) sacrifice some of this lightning speed in the interest of greater joinery versatility, such as cutting dovetails and louvers. And because the MatchMaker is the only one of these machines that mills tenons with the workpiece oriented horizontally, it will accommodate much longer workpieces more easily than any of the other machines.

The JDS Multi-Router Is in a Class by Itself

BY JOSEPH VAN BENTEN

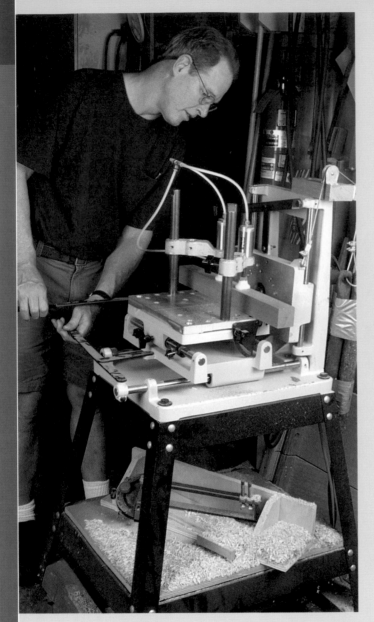

Price: $2,595

Source: www.thejdscompany.com

800-480-7269

Soon after I started to make furniture for a living, a quick and accurate way to make mortise-and-tenon joints became a necessity. In 1992, when I first saw the Multi-Router, made by the JDS Company, I bought one on the spot. This essentially is a small milling machine, powered by a portable router, with a table that moves on X and Y axes. The workpiece is clamped to this table. There is also a vertical table, to which the router (equipped with a spiral-upcut bit) is mounted horizontally, and this table provides a Z-axis motion.

The beauty of this machine is in its construction. The range of motion is supplied by linear roller bearings running on ground steel rods attached to ground aluminum tables. The table motion is absolutely effortless, and there is no discernible play in the bearings. The rods have flexible, movable collars and easy-to-adjust stops. In our shop, we clamp pieces as large as bed rails to the table with minimal outboard support, and we get joints that are uniform and repeatable.

The tables come from the factory drilled out with a series of holes to accommodate either manual or pneumatic clamps.

HANDLE CONTROLS EACH AXIS. With the Multi-Router, you have a separate handle for each of the X,Y, Z movements this machine will execute. Van Benten has used this machine in a production shop for more than 10 years, and he reports that the linear bearings on which the tables ride still work flawlessly.

Anyone accustomed to routers will feel at home with the Leigh and the Quick-Tenon. The MatchMaker and the WoodRat initially may seem a bit foreign, but the former's long levers and the latter's stock-feeding system offer exceptional cutter control.

The Leigh, which is easily stored away when not needed, and the WoodRat, which requires minimal floor space, will appeal

to woodworkers whose shop space is at a premium.

Such classic shop variables as available space and the scope or style of work that you do make it difficult to provide a one-size-fits-all recommendation. If you're thinking of buying one of these tools, you might want to remember this: All of these machines come with an unconditional

TEMPLATES GUIDE THE CUT. This machine comes with 42 different templates and inserts to use with various sizes of router bits. A steel stylus on the vertical router table traces the patterns, which are mounted on the horizontal table.

If you have a compressor, the air clamps are much faster and stronger than the manual clamps. They hold the work with unbelievable tenacity and facilitate very quick changing of parts.

The holes in the horizontal table allow instant setup for basic angle cuts. Hard plastic buttons fit in the holes in various patterns to create standard angles. We use this feature to mill the ends of large parts for multisided frames, after cutting the parts to approximate size on the bandsaw. The resulting joints are perfect, without the problems you get when using a tablesaw. The setup for angled cuts is not any more difficult than the setup for straight cuts.

Another feature of the Multi-Router is a stylus mounted on the vertical table that contacts and traces patterns mounted on the horizontal table. The stylus arrangement requires considerable setup time, and it does allow some objectionable flex in the cutting. Varying the pressure against the stylus can have an impact on the thickness of a milled part.

We use this machine to make mortises, tenons, and loose-spline joints. After 12 years of use, this machine is holding up beautifully. As a matter of fact, it has outlasted three routers.

30-day (or better) guarantee, which would give you a month in which to be your very own final arbiter.

★ Price estimates are from 2004.

MICHAEL STANDISH does custom trim carpentry and cabinetwork jobs in a garage shop just south of Boston, Massachusetts.

Credits

The New Best of Fine Woodworking Series

A collection of the best articles from the last ten years of Fine Woodworking

OTHER BOOKS IN THE SERIES

Designing Furniture
The Best of Fine Woodworking
From the editors of FWW
ISBN 1-56158-684-6
Product #070767
$17.95 U.S.
$25.95 Canada

Small Woodworking Shops
The Best of Fine Woodworking
From the editors of FWW
ISBN 1-56158-686-2
Product #070768
$17.95 U.S.
$25.95 Canada

Working with Routers
The Best of Fine Woodworking
From the editors of FWW
ISBN 1-56158-685-4
Product #070769
$17.95 U.S.
$25.95 Canada

Building Small Projects
The Best of Fine Woodworking
From the editors of FWW
ISBN 1-56158-730-3
Product #070791
$17.95 U.S.
$25.95 Canada

Designing and Building Cabinets
The Best of Fine Woodworking
From the editors of FWW
ISBN 1-56158-732-X
Product #070792
$17.95 U.S.
$25.95 Canada

Traditional Finishing Techniques
The Best of Fine Woodworking
From the editors of FWW
ISBN 1-56158-733-8
Product #070793
$17.95 U.S.
$25.95 Canada

Working with Handplanes
The Best of Fine Woodworking
From the editors of FWW
ISBN 1-56158-748-6
Product #070810
$17.95 U.S.
$25.95 Canada

Working with Tablesaws
The Best of Fine Woodworking
From the editors of FWW
ISBN 1-56158-749-4
Product #070811
$17.95 U.S.
$25.95 Canada

Workshop Machines
The Best of Fine Woodworking
From the editors of FWW
ISBN 1-56158-765-6
Product #070826
$17.95 U.S.
$25.95 Canada

Workstations and Tool Storage
The Best of Fine Woodworking
From the editors of FWW
ISBN 1-56158-785-0
Product #070838
$17.95 U.S.
$25.95 Canada

Traditional Projects
The Best of Fine Woodworking
From the editors of FWW
ISBN 1-56158-784-2
Product #070839
$17.95 U.S.
$25.95 Canada

Hand Tools
The Best of Fine Woodworking
From the editors of FWW
ISBN 1-56158-783-4
Product #070840
$17.95 U.S.
$25.95 Canada

Spray Finishing
The Best of Fine Woodworking
From the editors of FWW
ISBN 1-56158-829-6
Product #070875
$17.95 U.S.
$25.95 Canada

Selecting and Drying Wood
The Best of Fine Woodworking
From the editors of FWW
ISBN 1-56158-830-X
Product #070876
$17.95 U.S.
$25.95 Canada

The New Best of Fine Woodworking Slipcase Set Volume 1

Designing Furniture
Working with Routers
Small Woodworking Shops
Designing and Building Cabinets
Building Small Projects
Traditional Finishing Techniques

From the editors of FWW
ISBN 1-56158-736-2
Product #070808
$85.00 U.S./$120.00 Canada

The New Best of Fine Woodworking Slipcase Set Volume 2

Working with Handplanes
Workshop Machines
Working with Tablesaws
Selecting and Using Hand Tools
Traditional Projects
Workstations and Tool Storage

From the editors of FWW
ISBN 1-56158-747-8
Product #070809
$85.00 U.S./$120.00 Canada